LEAD YOUR BUSINESS AND TECHNOLOGY FROM INDIA

STRATEGIES FOR US AND EU BUSINESS OWNERS WHO WANT TO SET UP AND SCALE THEIR BUSINESSES FROM INDIA.

RIKEN BHORANIA AND BHAUMIN CHORERA

Dedicated to all business owners from the United States and Europe who want to expand their businesses using India's untapped potential.

Contents

"Riken has become an important asset to our business. We greatly appreciate the partnership that has developed. He possesses an intuitive understanding of our project scopes and timelines and is adept at assessing our needs to create viable solutions. We rely heavily on Riken's valuable, time-saving suggestions and we feel his expertise ultimately positions us to effectively and efficiently grow our company. We highly recommend them if you are looking for exemplary communication, top-notch development solutions, and leadership insight for your projects." - Mr. Dan Landes, CEO

"Bhaumin is extremely knowledgeable in systems and technology. He has helped us build a tailor-made solution for its unique business requirements. He also helped us staff so that we can slowly become self-reliant. I believe this shows Bhaumin's honesty and transparency in dealing with customers. We continue to engage with Ascetic as we write this feedback." - Mr. Asit Beesen, CEO

"We want to thank the team at Ascetic Business Solution, specifically Riken and Bhaumin, for their excellent service, professionalism, and most of all, their superior expertise. The team at Ascetic Business Solution deployed several detailed IT enhancements to our operational platform that have greatly improved our functionality as a business. The careful planning, detailed workflow, safety, security, and protective measures they operate with, have been paramount to us. We highly recommend Ascetic Business Solution and their services. We are continuing with many more projects with them and look forward to a long working relationship." - Mr. Brian Hoynowski, CEO

"Bhaumin, I really appreciate your expertise in Odoo, together with the splendid collaboration and your aim to help! Whilst you are a few thousand miles away, we can keep short communication lines and maintain good cooperation. We are very happy with the partnership and will certainly continue to work with Ascetic Business Solution LLP in the future!" - Mr.

Roeland Vandecan, Director

"I feel privileged to recommend the services of the Ascetic Business Solution firm. We have been working with them for the last five years, and they have always done everything with high quality and detailed, they are keen to meet all the expectations. His responsiveness to urgent matters makes them unique, always makes your requirements on time." - Mr. Oscar Martínez, CEO & Co-founder

"We are a startup and were searching a flexible and professional supporter and developer. The new partner should guide us in continuing the development of our web access and platform, pre-developed by another leading Odoo developer in Switzerland. Ascetic was recommended to us by a third party as a trustful and professional partner. Within a short time, we successfully transferred the development tasks to Ascetic. With the help of Ascetic, we are now fully in control. We gained trust in Ascetic. A reliable development partner is crucial for the success of our pendent capital increase and beyond." - Mr. Ralph Rechsteiner, Founder.

"It is a great pleasure to work with Riken and Bhaumin, and all the Ascetic Business Solution team. They have a structured approach, it is very professional and reassuring. They are very efficient and flexible." - Mr. Benoit BLANCHER, CDO

"Ascetic Business Solution was recommended to us by a friend. Riken and his team have proven themselves to be very helpful in implementing Odoo for our business. Riken is very knowledgeable in the software, and for any question we ask him about any configuration or customization we need, he always is quick to find a solution for us. If you are looking to setup work in India with your company, I would recommend Riken and Ascetic." - Mr. Todd Weaver, Co-founder.

"Soon after we started implementing Odoo, we came into contact with Bhaumin. He has been instrumental in customizing Odoo to our specific needs, in such a way that working with Odoo for us is far more efficient than it would have been without the software Ascetic Business Solution created for us. In this process, Ascetic has proven to be both affordable and reliable. If you need help with Odoo, Ascetic is a trustworthy partner to work with and we fully recommend them." - Mr. Steven Kroesbergen, CEO

"We have been working with Ascetic for some time now, after a disappointing experience with a different Odoo service provider. Ascetic have proven to be highly professional and competent with both a deep understanding of Odoo, a high technical level, and very transparent in the way they work. We are looking forward to a long and fruitful relationship." - Mr. Hezi Stern, Product Owner

"Riken and his team at Ascetic Business Solution LLP been instrumental in helping us switch to teach setup. Riken has been very helpful in implementing any changes we need, or questions we had during the setup process. If you're looking to switch to geting help from India partner, I highly recommend Ascetic Business Solution" - Mr. Josh Martin, CEO

"Riken and the Ascetic Business Solution team consistently go above and beyond our expectations. Their understanding of tech and their innate ability to easily interpret our vision allows them to create viable solutions, quickly. This translates to efficient and streamlined efforts on both sides of the project. Even with our aggressive timelines and scope deviations, they have the bandwidth to adjust and react effectively. Our company has really come to rely on them for their expert development solutions." - Mr. Dan Landes, CEO

"It is a pleasure to work with you and your team. I would like to emphasize your team's professionalism in terms of work execution, the tasks was completed in time and exactly as required. I would also like to highlight the level of responsiveness you've shown, prompt and clear communication is

always the key to success. We are looking forward to more common projects together." - Miss. Jane Davies, Project Manager

"We have been working with Ascetic business Solution for over a year, which has been an exceptional experience. Not only have they solved our requirements, but they have made us many custom developments, especially in the eCommerce module. Since we began working with them, the relationship has been permanent, and their extensive knowledge is impressive. We have had the opportunity to work hand in hand with Bhaumin whose professionalism, high level of responsiveness and prompt and clear communication skills have exceeded our expectations." - Miss. Genesis Alvarez, Project Manager

"As a small but growing business in the wake of Covid, we found itself out of control and in deep trouble. Due to a confluence of circumstances, our systems were failing, turnover was high, cash was tight, and we had lost the ability to keep projects moving. The situation was demotivating and frustrating for our team, and despair was setting in. After months of working with our previous development team, we were not making progress. They were not listening to our needs and seemed to be only able to deliver half-baked solutions that were not taking us forward. We desperately needed help. I connected with Riken and Bhaumin at Ascetic Business Solution, who seemed to understand our situation and offered help. These two guys have proven to be genuine, knowledgeable, and helpful. They listen to me and, more importantly, provide honest feedback based on their experience. I thoroughly enjoy working with them, and together, we have begun to make the changes needed to bring hope back to us and take us into the future.

Despite being half a world away, we meet weekly to review assignments, and Bhaumin keeps me updated with daily progress reports. I could not be happier working with Ascetic Business Solution and encourage anyone who finds their company in a similar place to give them a try." - Mr. Anthony Clayton, CEO/Owner

Foreword

Welcome to the Land of Opportunities

• xi •

Overview of India's potential

Booming Economy

India's economy is on a remarkable trajectory, making headlines with its rapid growth and dynamic business environment. With a GDP growth rate consistently above 7%, India has positioned itself as one of the fastest-growing major economies in the world. This robust economic expansion is fueled by a combination of factors, including a young and energetic workforce, a burgeoning middle class, and significant investments in infrastructure and technology.

Recent research highlights that India's economy is expected to become the third-largest globally by 2030, trailing only the United States and China. The country's strategic location, coupled with its diverse market, makes it an attractive destination for foreign direct investment (FDI). In 2023 alone, India attracted over $85 billion in FDI, underscoring its status as a global investment hotspot.

The government's pro-business policies, such as the Make in India initiative and various reforms to ease doing business, have further enhanced India's appeal. These initiatives aim to transform India into a global manufacturing hub, encouraging both domestic and international companies to set up operations in the country. The ease of doing business has significantly improved, with India climbing steadily in the World Bank's Ease of Doing Business rankings.

Moreover, India's digital economy is booming, with projections indicating that it could reach $1 trillion by 2025. The rapid adoption of digital technologies, coupled with a supportive regulatory environment, has fostered a vibrant startup ecosystem. Cities like Ahmedabad, Bengaluru,

Hyderabad, and Pune have emerged as major tech hubs, attracting talent and investment from around the world.

Abundant Talent

India's talent pool is one of its most compelling assets. The country produces over a million engineers annually, thanks to its extensive network of technical institutions. Among these are the prestigious Indian Institutes of Technology (IITs) and Indian Institutes of Management (IIMs), which are renowned for their rigorous academic programs and producing top-tier talent.

These institutions are not only celebrated in India but have gained international recognition for their excellence. Graduates from IITs and IIMs are highly sought after by global companies, and many hold leadership positions in top organizations worldwide.

The impact of India's talent pool extends beyond engineering and management. The country is also a powerhouse in sectors like information technology, pharmaceuticals, and biotechnology. India's IT sector, in particular, has been a major contributor to the global tech landscape, with companies like Tata Consultancy Services (TCS), Infosys, and Wipro leading the charge.

Recent advancements in research and development have further enhanced India's capabilities. The country is investing heavily in cutting-edge fields such as artificial intelligence (AI), machine learning, and robotics. These investments are not only driving innovation but also creating new opportunities for skilled professionals.

India's education system is also evolving to meet the demands of a rapidly changing world. Initiatives to integrate AI and advanced technologies into school curriculums are implemented, ensuring that the next generation is equipped with the skills needed to thrive in the digital age. This focus on STEM (Science, Technology, Engineering, and Mathematics) education is laying the foundation for a future-ready workforce.

Innovative Education

Education in India is undergoing a transformative phase, with a strong emphasis on innovation and technology. The government's National

Education Policy (NEP) 2020 aims to overhaul the education system, making it more holistic, flexible, and aligned with the needs of the 21st century.

One of the key aspects of this transformation is the integration of AI and other advanced technologies into the curriculum. Schools across the country are incorporating AI, coding, and data science into their teaching methodologies, preparing students for the future job market. This early exposure to technology not only fosters critical thinking and problem-solving skills but also ignites a passion for innovation.

Higher education institutions are also embracing change. Universities and colleges are partnering with industry leaders to offer specialized programs and certifications in emerging technologies. These collaborations ensure that the curriculum remains relevant and up-to-date with industry standards. Students have access to state-of-the-art facilities and resources, enabling them to gain hands-on experience in their chosen fields.

Furthermore, India is witnessing a rise in the number of innovation and incubation centers within educational institutions. These centers serve as breeding grounds for new ideas and entrepreneurial ventures. Students are encouraged to explore their creativity and develop solutions to real-world problems. The success of startups emerging from these centers is a testament to the innovative spirit nurtured within India's educational ecosystem.

Global Leadership

Indians are making their mark on the global stage, demonstrating exceptional leadership and expertise across various industries. From Silicon Valley to Wall Street, Indian professionals are at the helm of some of the world's most influential companies.

In addition to corporate leadership, Indian professionals are also excelling in academia, research, and public service. Indian-origin scientists, researchers, and academicians are making significant contributions to global knowledge and innovation. Their work in fields such as medicine, engineering, and social sciences is shaping the future and addressing some of the world's most pressing challenges.

The Indian diaspora plays a crucial role in this global leadership narrative. With over 30 million Indians living abroad, the diaspora serves as a bridge between India and the rest of the world. They bring with them a wealth of knowledge, experience, and cultural understanding, fostering stronger international collaborations and partnerships.

India's commitment to fostering leadership extends to its domestic policies as well. The government and various organizations are implementing programs to identify and nurture future leaders from diverse backgrounds. Initiatives aimed at promoting gender equality and inclusivity in leadership roles are gaining momentum, ensuring that the leadership pipeline is both broad and deep.

Conclusion

India's potential is immense, driven by a booming economy, an abundant talent pool, innovative education, and global leadership. The country's rapid growth and dynamic business environment make it a prime destination for global businesses seeking new opportunities. With a strong emphasis on STEM education and cutting-edge technologies, India is preparing its workforce for the future, ensuring sustained innovation and growth. As Indian professionals continue to make their mark on the global stage, the country's influence and impact will only continue to grow. Embracing India's potential means tapping into a vast reservoir of talent, creativity, and leadership, ready to shape the future of business and technology on a global scale.

Preface

Why this book is essential for business owners

•

High Demand for Indian Professionals in the USA and Europe

The global business landscape is evolving rapidly, with Indian professionals emerging as key players in the fields of technology, software development, and innovation. The demand for skilled Indian professionals in the USA and Europe is at an all-time high. Companies are eager to tap into this vast pool of talent, known for their expertise, dedication, and innovative mindset. However, despite this high demand, accessing Indian talent is not as straightforward as it seems.

Tough Immigration Rules and Limited Access to Talent

One of the significant hurdles for business owners in the USA and Europe is navigating the stringent immigration laws. These laws often make it difficult for companies to bring in skilled Indian professionals. The process is cumbersome, time-consuming, and uncertain. As a result, many businesses struggle to access the talent they desperately need to stay competitive in the market. This book provides insights into overcoming these challenges by establishing a presence in India, allowing businesses to leverage local talent without the constraints of immigration laws.

Outsourcing: A Solution with Limited Control

Outsourcing has been a common strategy for many companies looking to cut costs and access global talent. However, outsourcing comes with its own set of challenges. One of the primary issues is the lack of control. When you outsource your projects, you often lose the ability to oversee the work closely, leading to potential quality issues, communication gaps, and delays. This book highlights why setting up your own R&D center in India is a more sustainable and effective solution. It provides you with complete control over your operations, ensuring that your projects align perfectly with your vision and standards.

Establishing Operations in India: A Sustainable Long-Term Solution

In today's competitive business environment, long-term sustainability is crucial. Establishing operations in India offers a robust and enduring solution to various challenges faced by business owners in the USA and Europe. By setting up R&D centers and operational hubs in India, companies can not only access top-tier talent but also create a strategic foothold in one of the world's fastest-growing economies. This approach allows businesses to innovate, grow, and scale without the constant worry of immigration issues or the limitations of outsourcing.

Moreover, having a dedicated team in India means you can develop products and solutions that are designed and developed locally. This not only enhances your brand's reputation but also instills a sense of pride and ownership among your employees and customers. The trend is shifting towards companies being proud to announce that their products are developed in India, reflecting a global mindset and a commitment to quality.

Growing Your Business and Ensuring Long-Term Success

Businesses that have established their operations and technology centers in India have witnessed remarkable growth. There are numerous examples of companies that were on the brink of bankruptcy but managed to turn things around by leveraging the talent and resources available in India. This book provides case studies and real-life examples of how businesses have not only survived but thrived by investing in India.

By setting up your operations in India, you can achieve exponential growth. The cost savings, access to a vast pool of skilled professionals, and the ability to innovate and develop cutting-edge solutions make India an ideal destination for business expansion. This book serves as a comprehensive guide for business owners looking to explore this opportunity, providing practical advice, strategies, and best practices to ensure a successful transition and long-term growth.

Conclusion

In conclusion, this book is an essential resource for business owners in the USA and Europe who are looking to stay ahead in the competitive market. It addresses the pain points of accessing Indian talent, the limitations of outsourcing, and the challenges of immigration laws. By establishing operations in India, business owners can ensure long-term sustainability, complete control over their projects, and the ability to innovate and grow their business exponentially. This book provides the roadmap to achieve these goals, helping you leverage the full potential of Indian talent and resources to lead your business and technology to new heights.

Chapter 1: Discovering India's Untapped Potential

India: The New Business Frontier

Introduction to India's growing economy

Strategic advantages of operating in India

Talent Pool Galore

Overview of India's skilled workforce

Introduction to India's growing economy

India's economy is a fascinating tapestry woven with diverse threads of innovation, technology, tradition, and growth. As the world's fifth-largest economy, India offers a myriad of opportunities for businesses worldwide. This section delves into the core aspects that make India the new business frontier, focusing on its vibrant startup ecosystem, digital revolution, renewable energy ambitions, and more.

The Startup Hub: A Breeding Ground for Innovation

India's startup ecosystem is a testament to the country's entrepreneurial spirit and technological prowess. With over 60,000 startups, India stands as the third-largest startup ecosystem globally. This dynamic environment fosters innovation across various sectors, from fintech and edtech to health tech and agritech.

The government's initiatives, such as Startup India, have played a pivotal role in nurturing this ecosystem. These initiatives provide startups with the necessary support, including funding, mentorship, and infrastructure. Furthermore, India's vast pool of talented engineers, developers, and entrepreneurs fuels the growth of these startups, making it an attractive destination for foreign investors.

Foreign business owners can tap into this vibrant ecosystem to collaborate, invest, or even acquire innovative startups, thereby gaining a competitive edge in their respective markets. The continuous influx of venture capital and private equity investments highlights the confidence global investors have in India's startup potential.

Leading the Digital Revolution

India is at the forefront of the digital revolution, leading the world in digital transactions. In 2021 alone, India recorded over 40 billion digital transactions, showcasing the country's rapid adoption of digital technologies. The Unified Payments Interface (UPI) has revolutionized the payment landscape, making transactions seamless and secure.

This digital transformation extends beyond payments. The Indian government's Digital India initiative aims to empower citizens and businesses through digital technologies. From e-governance and digital infrastructure to internet connectivity and cybersecurity, India is building a robust digital foundation.

For businesses, this means a conducive environment for digital innovation. Companies can leverage India's digital infrastructure to expand their operations, reach new customers, and streamline processes. The tech-savvy consumer base, coupled with the government's push for digital inclusion, creates a fertile ground for digital businesses to thrive.

Embracing Renewable Energy: A Sustainable Future

India is making significant strides in renewable energy, positioning itself as a global leader. As the third-largest producer of renewable energy, India is committed to achieving 450 GW of renewable energy capacity by 2030. This ambitious goal underscores the country's dedication to sustainable development.

The renewable energy sector in India encompasses solar, wind, hydro, and biomass energy. The government's favorable policies, incentives, and investment in renewable infrastructure have attracted global players to the Indian market. For instance, India's solar energy capacity has grown exponentially, making it one of the largest solar markets in the world.

Businesses looking to invest in sustainable energy solutions will find India a lucrative market. The availability of renewable resources, combined with government support, offers immense potential for growth and innovation. Moreover, companies can benefit from cost-effective energy solutions, reducing their carbon footprint and enhancing their corporate social responsibility initiatives.

The Gig Economy: A Flexible Workforce

India's gig economy is rapidly expanding, with over 15 million people contributing to this sector. The gig economy includes freelancers, part-time workers, and independent contractors who provide various services, from ride-sharing and food delivery to digital marketing and software development.

The flexibility and cost-effectiveness of the gig economy make it an attractive option for businesses. Companies can access a diverse talent pool without the long-term commitment of traditional employment. This model allows businesses to scale their operations efficiently, respond to market demands, and reduce overhead costs.

The rise of digital platforms and the increasing acceptance of remote work have further fueled the growth of the gig economy. For international businesses, this means access to a skilled and adaptable workforce, capable of driving innovation and efficiency.

Conclusion

India's growing economy is a beacon of opportunity for global business owners. The country's vibrant startup ecosystem, digital revolution, renewable energy ambitions, and the gig economy create a dynamic and promising business environment. By tapping into India's untapped potential, businesses can innovate, expand, and thrive in the global market. This subchapter has outlined key areas where India's economic growth presents unparalleled opportunities, setting the stage for deeper exploration in the chapters to come.

Strategic Advantages of Operating in India

India is a land of immense opportunities, characterized by its robust economic growth, diverse talent pool, and rapidly evolving business environment. For business owners in the USA and Europe, establishing operations in India offers a strategic edge that can significantly impact their global competitiveness. This subchapter explores the strategic advantages of operating in India and the potential consequences of not leveraging these opportunities.

1. Access to a Vast and Skilled Talent Pool

India boasts one of the largest and youngest workforces in the world. With over 600 million people under the age of 25, the country offers a vast pool of skilled professionals across various industries. Indian universities produce millions of graduates annually, many of whom specialize in fields like engineering, information technology, and management.

Strategic Advantage: Business owners can tap into this rich talent pool to drive innovation, improve productivity, and gain a competitive edge. India's emphasis on STEM (Science, Technology, Engineering, and Mathematics) education ensures a steady supply of highly skilled professionals ready to contribute to cutting-edge projects.

Consequence of Missing Out: Failing to leverage this talent pool means missing out on the opportunity to enhance your business's capabilities. Competitors who capitalize on India's skilled workforce will have the advantage of faster innovation cycles, higher productivity, and better cost-efficiency, potentially outpacing businesses that do not.

2. Cost-Effective Operations

India offers a cost-effective environment for business operations. The cost of labor, infrastructure, and resources is significantly lower compared to Western countries. This cost advantage extends to various sectors, including manufacturing, IT services, and research and development.

Strategic Advantage: Establishing operations in India allows businesses to reduce their operational costs while maintaining high-quality standards. This cost-efficiency enables companies to allocate resources more effectively, invest in innovation, and offer competitive pricing to their customers.

Consequence of Missing Out: Businesses that do not take advantage of India's cost-effective environment may struggle to compete on price and profitability. Higher operational costs in their home countries can limit their ability to invest in growth and innovation, leaving them vulnerable to more agile and cost-efficient competitors.

3. Strategic Geographic Location

India's strategic location in South Asia makes it an ideal hub for businesses looking to expand their reach across Asia, the Middle East, and Africa. The country's proximity to key markets and its well-developed transportation infrastructure facilitate seamless trade and logistics operations.

Strategic Advantage: By establishing a presence in India, businesses can efficiently serve a broader market base. India's extensive network of ports, airports, and highways ensures smooth supply chain operations, reducing transit times and costs.

Consequence of Missing Out: Companies that do not utilize India's strategic location may face higher logistics costs and longer delivery times, impacting their ability to compete in global markets. Competitors with a strategic presence in India will have the advantage of faster market access and improved supply chain efficiency.

4. Growing Domestic Market

India's domestic market is one of the fastest-growing in the world. With a burgeoning middle class and increasing disposable incomes, consumer demand is rising across various sectors, from consumer goods and retail to technology and healthcare.

Strategic Advantage: Businesses that establish operations in India can directly tap into this growing domestic market. By understanding local consumer preferences and trends, companies can tailor their products and services to meet the needs of Indian consumers, driving sales and market share.

Consequence of Missing Out: Failing to enter the Indian market means missing out on a significant revenue opportunity. Competitors who establish a foothold in India will benefit from the growing consumer demand, while businesses that remain absent may struggle to achieve similar growth rates and market penetration.

5. Innovation and R&D Opportunities

India is emerging as a global hub for innovation and research and development (R&D). The country's focus on technology and innovation is supported by a vibrant startup ecosystem, world-class educational institutions, and government initiatives promoting R&D activities.

Strategic Advantage: Setting up R&D centers in India allows businesses to leverage local expertise and innovation capabilities. Companies can collaborate with Indian startups, universities, and research institutions to drive technological advancements and develop innovative solutions.

Consequence of Missing Out: Businesses that do not invest in R&D in India may fall behind in technological innovation. Competitors who harness India's innovation ecosystem will have the advantage of developing cutting-edge products and solutions, gaining a significant market edge.

Conclusion

India offers a multitude of strategic advantages for business owners from the USA and Europe. Access to a skilled talent pool, cost-effective operations, a strategic geographic location, a growing domestic market, and abundant innovation opportunities make India an attractive destination for business expansion. However, failing to leverage these advantages can result in missed opportunities, reduced competitiveness, and slower growth.

By understanding and capitalizing on India's untapped potential, businesses can not only enhance their global presence but also secure a sustainable and competitive future. The insights provided in this book will guide you in making informed decisions and successfully establishing your operations in India, ensuring you stay ahead in the ever-evolving global market.

Overview of India's skilled workforce

The Roots of Talent Pool Galore

Historical Foundation

The emphasis on education in India is not a recent phenomenon. Historically, India has always valued learning and scholarship, with ancient universities that attracted students from around the world. Fast forward to 2024, India boasts over 39,000 colleges and 900 universities, making it one of the largest higher education systems globally.

Modern Education System

The modern Indian education system has kept pace with global standards, offering a wide range of disciplines. From engineering to medicine, and from the arts to management, Indian universities provide comprehensive training. The Indian Institutes of Technology (IITs) and Indian Institutes of Management (IIMs) are globally recognized for their excellence. For instance, the IITs have produced numerous CEOs of Fortune 500 companies, underscoring the quality of education and the caliber of graduates they produce.

Government Initiatives

The Indian government has been proactive in fostering a skilled workforce. Initiatives like 'Skill India' and 'Digital India' aim to enhance the skill set of the population, ensuring they are prepared for the demands of the modern workplace. These programs focus on various sectors, including IT, manufacturing, and services, providing training to millions of individuals.

The Advantages of India's Talent Pool

India's talent pool offers numerous advantages that make it a prime destination for businesses looking to leverage skilled professionals.

Diverse Skill Set

India's workforce is incredibly diverse, encompassing a wide range of skills and expertise. From software development to biotechnology, and from finance to creative industries, Indian professionals excel in various fields. This diversity allows businesses to find the exact talent they need without having to look far and wide.

English Proficiency

ne of India's standout advantages is the high level of English proficiency among its professionals. English is a primary medium of instruction in many schools and universities, which means that Indian graduates are often fluent in English. This proficiency facilitates smooth communication and collaboration with international teams, making it easier for businesses to integrate Indian talent into their operations.

Cost Efficiency

While the focus is on quality, the cost advantage cannot be ignored. Hiring skilled professionals in India often comes at a fraction of the cost compared to hiring in the USA or Europe. This cost efficiency allows businesses to allocate resources more effectively, investing in innovation and growth rather than just operational expenses.

Work Ethic and Adaptability

Indian professionals are known for their strong work ethic and adaptability. They are often willing to go the extra mile to meet deadlines and ensure the success of projects. Additionally, their ability to adapt to different cultural and business environments makes them valuable assets to any international team.

Expanding the Talent Pool: Future Prospects

The future of India's talent pool looks promising, with continuous expansion and improvement in quality.

Increasing Enrollment

There has been a significant increase in enrollment in higher education in India. According to recent statistics, the Gross Enrollment Ratio (GER) in higher education has been steadily rising, reaching 27.1% in 2021. This increase means more graduates entering the workforce each year, further bolstering the talent pool.

Focus on STEM

India is placing a strong emphasis on STEM (Science, Technology, Engineering, and Mathematics) education. Initiatives like the Atal Innovation Mission and numerous scholarships for STEM students aim to nurture innovation and research. This focus is expected to produce a new generation of highly skilled professionals ready to tackle the challenges of the future.

Tech-Savvy Youth

India's youth are incredibly tech-savvy, with a strong inclination towards technology and innovation. The country is home to one of the largest pools of tech developers and IT professionals globally. Cities like Ahmedabad, Bangalore, Hyderabad, and Pune are hubs of tech activity, housing numerous startups and tech giants. This tech-savvy workforce is driving India's reputation as a global IT powerhouse.

Global Impact

The impact of India's skilled workforce is felt worldwide. Indian professionals are present in leading roles across various industries globally. Their success stories highlight the potential and caliber of India's talent pool.

In conclusion, India's skilled workforce is a testament to the country's commitment to education and excellence. The roots of this talent pool are deep, its advantages are numerous, and its future prospects are bright. For businesses in the USA and Europe, tapping into this talent pool offers a strategic advantage that can drive innovation, efficiency, and growth. By understanding and leveraging India's talent pool, businesses can not only benefit themselves but also contribute to the global economy's overall development.

Chapter 2: Navigating the Indian Business Landscape

Understanding the Indian Market

Cultural nuances and business etiquette

Key industries and opportunities in India

Legal and Regulatory Framework

Essential laws and regulations

Navigating the bureaucracy

Cultural nuances and business etiquette

The Heartbeat of Indian Culture

Understanding the cultural nuances of India is crucial for successful business collaboration. India, with its rich tapestry of traditions, languages, and customs, offers a unique and vibrant business environment. Here are some key cultural aspects to keep in mind:

Respect for Hierarchy

In India, respect for hierarchy is deeply ingrained in both personal and professional settings. This can be traced back to the family structure, where the eldest family member is often regarded with utmost respect. Similarly, in the business world, decisions are typically made by senior executives. Acknowledging and respecting this hierarchy can facilitate smoother interactions and decision-making processes.

Personal Relationships

Building personal relationships is fundamental to business in India. Unlike in some Western cultures where business relationships might remain strictly professional, in India, getting to know your business partners on a personal level is often seen as a key component of successful collaboration. This might involve socializing outside of formal business meetings, sharing meals, and discussing topics beyond business.

Diverse Communication Styles

India is a land of diverse languages and communication styles. While English is widely spoken and used in business, understanding regional languages and the non-verbal cues can be beneficial. For instance, a head nod might mean agreement or simply acknowledgment, depending on the context. Paying attention to these subtleties can help avoid misunderstandings.

Business Etiquette Essentials

Navigating the Indian business landscape requires an understanding of specific etiquette to ensure respectful and effective interactions.

Greetings and Introductions

In India, greetings often blend traditional and modern practices. A common greeting is "Namaste," where you press your palms together at chest level with a slight bow. However, handshakes are also common, especially in urban areas and among business professionals. It's best to start with a handshake and follow the lead of your Indian counterpart.

Dress Code

Business attire in India tends to be formal, especially in corporate settings. Men typically wear suits and ties, while women may wear suits, saris, or formal dresses. In more relaxed or creative industries, business casual attire might be acceptable, but it's always better to err on the side of formality, especially for initial meetings.

Punctuality and Time Management

Punctuality is valued in Indian business culture, but it's also important to be flexible. While you should aim to be on time, understand that meetings may not always start promptly, and schedules can change. Patience and adaptability are key traits to have when doing business in India.

Best Practices for Effective Collaboration

To effectively collaborate with Indian businesses, it's important to blend respect for cultural norms with strategic business practices.

Building Trust and Rapport

Trust is the cornerstone of business relationships in India. Invest time in building trust with your Indian counterparts. This might involve multiple meetings, social interactions, and demonstrating a genuine interest in their culture and practices. Trust, once established, can lead to long-term and fruitful business relationships.

Decision-Making Process

The decision-making process in India can be slower than in some Western countries. This is partly due to the hierarchical structure and the need for consensus among various stakeholders. Be prepared for multiple rounds of discussions and negotiations. Demonstrating patience and respect for this process can facilitate smoother collaborations.

Adaptability and Open-mindedness

India's business environment is dynamic and rapidly evolving. Being adaptable and open-minded is crucial for success. Whether it's adapting to different communication styles, being flexible with time management, or understanding local market conditions, an adaptable approach will serve you well.

Real-World Example

Consider the case of a multinational technology company entering the Indian market. The company's executives spent months building relationships with local partners, understanding cultural nuances, and adapting their business practices to align with local expectations. They learned to navigate the hierarchical decision-making process and invested time in social interactions outside of formal business meetings. This approach not only facilitated a successful market entry but also established a strong foundation for long-term growth and collaboration.

In conclusion, understanding and respecting India's cultural nuances and business etiquette is essential for effective collaboration. By appreciating the hierarchical structure, investing in personal relationships, and being adaptable, business owners from the USA and Europe can navigate the Indian business landscape with confidence. This understanding not only fosters respect and trust but also paves the way for successful and sustainable business ventures in one of the world's most dynamic markets.

Key Industries and Opportunities in India

The IT Powerhouse

India's Information Technology (IT) sector is nothing short of a global phenomenon. Over the past few decades, India has established itself as a leader in the IT industry, providing a wide range of services from software development to IT consulting.

The Growth Story

The IT industry in India has seen exponential growth. In the fiscal year 2021-2022, the IT sector contributed approximately $194 billion to India's GDP, showcasing its significant role in the economy. Companies like Tata Consultancy Services (TCS), Infosys, and Wipro are not only Indian giants but also global leaders, serving clients all over the world.

Skilled Workforce

India's IT workforce is among the most skilled in the world. With a strong emphasis on STEM (Science, Technology, Engineering, and Mathematics) education, India produces a vast number of IT graduates every year. The country's IT professionals are renowned for their technical expertise, problem-solving skills, and ability to deliver high-quality solutions. For instance, TCS, one of India's largest IT firms, employs over 500,000 people worldwide, illustrating the scale and capability of India's IT talent pool.

Cost-Effective Solutions

One of the primary reasons global businesses turn to India for IT services is the cost advantage. The ability to provide high-quality services at competitive prices makes India an attractive destination for outsourcing IT projects. This cost-effectiveness, combined with the availability of skilled professionals, allows businesses to achieve their technological goals while optimizing their budgets.

Services Sector: A Diverse Landscape

India's services sector is a diverse and dynamic landscape, offering a multitude of opportunities for international businesses. This sector spans across various industries, including finance, healthcare, education, and tourism.

Financial Services

India's financial services sector is robust and rapidly growing. With a focus on digital transformation, the sector is evolving to meet the needs of a tech-savvy population. Digital banking, fintech innovations, and insurance services are areas with significant potential. Companies like Paytm and PolicyBazaar are examples of how Indian firms are revolutionizing financial services through technology.

Healthcare Services

The healthcare sector in India is another area ripe with opportunities. With a growing middle class and increasing health awareness, there is a rising demand for quality healthcare services. Telemedicine, medical tourism, and health tech startups are transforming the landscape. For example, Practo, an Indian health tech startup, connects millions of patients with healthcare providers, demonstrating the potential of digital healthcare solutions in India.

Education Services

India's education sector is undergoing a digital revolution. Online learning platforms have seen unprecedented growth, especially during the COVID-19 pandemic. These platforms offer a range of courses and educational content, making quality education accessible to a broader audience. The demand for e-learning solutions provides ample opportunities for businesses looking to invest in the education sector.

Software Consulting: Driving Innovation

Software consulting is a critical component of India's IT and services sector, driving innovation and helping businesses transform digitally.

Innovation Hubs

Cities like Bangalore, Hyderabad, Ahmedabad and Pune are known as innovation hubs, housing numerous tech startups and multinational corporations. These cities offer a conducive environment for software consulting firms, providing access to top-tier talent and cutting-edge infrastructure. For instance, Bangalore, often referred to as the "Silicon Valley of India," is home to over 10,000 startups and numerous global tech giants.

Custom Solutions

Indian software consulting firms specialize in delivering custom solutions tailored to the unique needs of their clients. Whether it's developing enterprise software, providing cybersecurity services, or implementing AI and machine learning solutions, Indian firms excel in offering innovative and effective solutions. Companies like Infosys and Tech Mahindra are renowned for their expertise in software consulting, serving clients across various industries.

Global Impact

The impact of Indian software consulting extends far beyond its borders. Indian consultants work with businesses worldwide, helping them navigate digital transformation, improve operational efficiency, and drive innovation. This global reach underscores the importance of India's software consulting industry and its ability to deliver world-class solutions.

In conclusion, India's IT, services, and software consulting sectors present vast opportunities for business owners from the USA and Europe. By tapping into India's skilled workforce, leveraging cost-effective solutions, and embracing the innovative spirit of Indian firms, businesses can achieve significant growth and success. Understanding these key industries and the opportunities they offer is essential for navigating the Indian business landscape effectively.

Essential Laws and Regulations

Setting Up Business: Key Legal Requirements

Establishing a business in India involves navigating through several legal requirements. Understanding these essentials will ensure a smooth setup process and compliance with local regulations.

Business Structures

Choosing the right business structure is the first step. India offers several options:

- Private Limited Company: This is the most common structure for foreign businesses. It requires at least two directors and shareholders and offers limited liability protection.
- Limited Liability Partnership (LLP): An LLP provides the benefits of limited liability and allows partners to manage the business directly.
- Branch Office: Foreign companies can open a branch office to conduct business activities, subject to approval from the Reserve Bank of India (RBI).

Registration Process

Once you decide on the business structure, the next step is registration:

- Digital Signature Certificate (DSC): Required for signing documents electronically.
- Director Identification Number (DIN): Necessary for all directors of the company.
- Company Name Approval: The chosen name must be approved by the Registrar of Companies (RoC).
- Incorporation Documents: Submit the Memorandum of Association (MoA) and Articles of Association (AoA) to the RoC.

Compliance Requirements

After registration, maintaining compliance is crucial:

- Annual Returns: Companies must file annual returns with the Ministry of Corporate Affairs (MCA).
- Financial Statements: Audited financial statements must be filed annually.
- Board Meetings: Regular board meetings should be held and documented.

Employment Laws and Regulations

Understanding employment laws is vital for managing your workforce effectively and ensuring legal compliance.

Hiring Practices

- Employment Contracts: All employees should have a written contract outlining their terms of employment.

- Probation Period: Typically, new employees undergo a probation period ranging from three to six months.

Labor Laws

India has a comprehensive set of labor laws aimed at protecting employee rights:

- Minimum Wages Act: Ensures that workers receive a fair wage. The minimum wage varies by state and industry.
- Employees' Provident Fund (EPF): A mandatory savings scheme for employees, requiring contributions from both employers and employees.
- Employees' State Insurance (ESI): Provides health insurance and benefits to employees earning below a certain threshold.

Workplace Regulations

- Sexual Harassment: The Prevention of Sexual Harassment (POSH) Act mandates a safe working environment. Companies must have a policy in place and constitute an Internal Complaints Committee (ICC).
- Health and Safety: Adherence to health and safety standards is crucial. Regular audits and compliance checks should be conducted to ensure a safe workplace.

Taxation and Financial Regulations

Navigating India's taxation and financial regulations is essential for compliance and efficient business operations.

Tax Structure

India has a well-defined tax structure that includes both direct and indirect taxes:

- Corporate Tax: Companies incorporated in India are subject to corporate tax on their global income.
- Goods and Services Tax (GST): A comprehensive indirect tax that replaced multiple taxes. Businesses must register for GST and file regular returns.
- Withholding Tax: Also known as Tax Deducted at Source (TDS), this tax is withheld from payments made to vendors, contractors, and professionals.

Financial Reporting

- Indian Accounting Standards (Ind AS): These standards are aligned with the International Financial Reporting Standards (IFRS) and are mandatory for large companies.
- Audits: Annual financial audits are mandatory for all companies. An independent auditor must be appointed to review and certify the financial statements.

Real-World Example: Consider a US-based tech company looking to set up operations in India. They chose a Private Limited Company structure for its benefits. They went through the registration process, obtained the necessary DSC and DIN, and submitted the incorporation documents. They hired a local HR consultant to ensure compliance with Indian labor laws and implemented a POSH policy. For taxation, they registered for GST and ensured that their transactions complied with transfer pricing regulations. By understanding and adhering to these laws, the company successfully established its presence in India, leveraging the local talent pool and growing its business.

In conclusion, understanding the essential laws and regulations in India is crucial for establishing and running a business smoothly. From choosing the right business structure and complying with employment laws to navigating the tax landscape, being well-informed will help you avoid legal pitfalls and ensure a successful venture in the Indian market.

Navigating the Bureaucracy

Understanding the Bureaucratic Landscape

Navigating the bureaucratic landscape in India can seem daunting, but with the right approach, it becomes manageable and even advantageous.

Complex but Improving

India's bureaucracy is often viewed as complex, with multiple layers of regulations and approvals. However, significant improvements have been made in recent years to simplify the process. Initiatives like 'Digital India' and 'Make in India' aim to reduce red tape and make it easier for businesses to operate. For instance, the introduction of the Goods and Services Tax (GST) has streamlined the indirect tax system, replacing multiple taxes with a single, unified tax.

Key Agencies and Departments

- Several government agencies and departments play crucial roles in the business setup process:
- Ministry of Corporate Affairs (MCA): Handles company registration and compliance.
- Reserve Bank of India (RBI): Manages foreign exchange regulations and approvals.
- Central Board of Direct Taxes (CBDT): Oversees direct taxation.
- Central Board of Indirect Taxes and Customs (CBIC): Manages indirect taxation, including GST.

Understanding the functions of these agencies and maintaining regular communication with them can significantly ease the bureaucratic process.

Practical Steps for Navigating Bureaucracy

Here are some practical steps to help you navigate the bureaucratic maze effectively:

1. Hire Local Expertise

One of the most effective ways to handle bureaucracy is to hire local experts. Chartered accountants, legal advisors, and compliance managers familiar with Indian regulations can guide you through the necessary procedures. For example, when a US-based tech firm wanted to establish a presence in India, they hired a local consulting firm to handle all their registration and compliance needs, which saved them time and ensured everything was done correctly.

2. Leverage Digital Platforms

India has made significant strides in digitalizing bureaucratic processes. Platforms like the MCA's online portal allow for the digital submission of documents, reducing the need for physical paperwork. Similarly, the GST portal facilitates online tax filings and payments. Utilizing these digital platforms can streamline your interactions with government agencies.

3. Understand Key Procedures

Familiarize yourself with key procedures that are essential for business operations:

- Company Incorporation: Registering your business with the MCA, obtaining a Director Identification Number (DIN), and getting your company name approved.
- Tax Registrations: Registering for GST, obtaining a Permanent Account Number (PAN), and a Tax Deduction and Collection Account Number (TAN).

- Employment Regulations: Complying with labor laws, including Provident Fund (PF) and Employees' State Insurance (ESI) registrations.

By understanding these procedures and preparing the necessary documentation in advance, you can expedite the setup process.

Overcoming Common Challenges

Even with the best preparation, you might encounter some challenges. Here's how to overcome common bureaucratic hurdles:

Delays and Follow-ups

Bureaucratic processes can sometimes be slow. It's essential to follow up regularly with the concerned departments to ensure your applications are moving forward. For instance, when an international retail company faced delays in getting their Foreign Direct Investment (FDI) approval, consistent follow-ups and direct communication with the Department for Promotion of Industry and Internal Trade (DPIIT) helped expedite the process.

Clear Communication

Clear and precise communication with government officials can make a significant difference. Always ensure your applications and documents are complete and error-free. If there are any discrepancies, address them promptly to avoid delays.

Utilize Government Support

Take advantage of government schemes and support initiatives designed to help businesses. Programs like 'Startup India' offer various incentives, including tax benefits, easier compliance, and financial support. When a European biotech firm entered the Indian market, they leveraged the 'Startup India' program to gain faster clearances and financial incentives, easing their entry into the Indian market.

Network and Collaborate

Building a network of local business contacts can provide valuable insights and assistance. Join industry associations, attend business forums, and connect with other entrepreneurs who have experience navigating the bureaucracy. Their experiences and advice can help you avoid common pitfalls and find efficient solutions.

In conclusion, while navigating the bureaucracy in India might seem challenging, it is entirely manageable with the right approach. By hiring local expertise, leveraging digital platforms, understanding key procedures, and staying proactive, you can successfully navigate the bureaucratic landscape and set up your business smoothly. Remember, patience and persistence are your allies in this journey. With these strategies, you'll find that the Indian market is not only accessible but also full of exciting opportunities for growth and success.

Chapter 3: Setting Up Business in India

Establishing Your Presence

Step-by-step guide to setting up a business

Choosing the right location for your R&D center

Infrastructure and Logistics

Overview of India's infrastructure

Step-by-Step Guide to Setting Up a Business

Initial Steps to Establish Your Business

Setting up a business in India involves several key steps to ensure compliance and smooth operations. Here's a step-by-step guide to help you navigate the process effectively.

1. Decide on a Business Structure

Choosing the right business structure is crucial as it affects your tax obligations, liability, and compliance requirements. Common structures include:

- Private Limited Company: Ideal for foreign businesses, offering limited liability and easy transfer of shares.
- Limited Liability Partnership (LLP): Combines the benefits of a partnership with limited liability protection.
- Branch Office: Allows foreign companies to conduct business in India with certain restrictions.

2. Obtain Digital Signature Certificate (DSC)

A DSC is necessary for signing electronic documents during the registration process. It ensures the authenticity and security of your digital communications.

3. Acquire Director Identification Number (DIN)

Directors of your company must obtain a DIN by submitting the required forms and identification documents to the Ministry of Corporate Affairs (MCA).

4. Reserve Your Company Name

Propose a unique name for your business and apply for name approval through the MCA portal. Ensure the name adheres to the naming guidelines provided by the MCA.

5. Register Your Company

Prepare the necessary documents, including the Memorandum of Association (MoA) and Articles of Association (AoA). Submit these documents along with the application for company registration on the MCA portal. Upon approval, you will receive a Certificate of Incorporation.

6. Apply for Permanent Account Number (PAN) and Tax Account Number (TAN)

Register for a PAN for tax purposes and a TAN for deducting and collecting tax at source. Both are mandatory for financial transactions and tax compliance.

7. Open a Bank Account

Open a corporate bank account in India to manage your business finances. You will need your incorporation certificate, PAN, and other documents as required by the bank.

Compliance and Operational Steps

Once your business is registered, the next steps involve compliance and setting up operational aspects to ensure smooth functioning.

1. Register for Goods and Services Tax (GST)

If your business turnover exceeds the threshold limit, you must register for GST. This involves filing an application online and obtaining a GSTIN (Goods and Services Tax Identification Number).

2. Obtain Other Necessary Licenses and Permits

Depending on your industry and location, you may need additional licenses and permits such as:

- Shops and Establishment License: For businesses operating in physical locations.
- Import Export Code (IEC): Required for businesses involved in international trade.
- Industry-Specific Licenses: Such as FSSAI for food businesses, or Drug License for pharmaceuticals.

3. Comply with Labor Laws

Ensure compliance with labor laws by registering for Employees' Provident Fund (EPF) and Employees' State Insurance (ESI). These are mandatory for businesses employing a certain number of people and provide social security benefits to employees.

4. Set Up Accounting and Compliance Systems

Implement robust accounting and compliance systems to manage finances, file taxes, and ensure regulatory compliance. Hiring a local accountant or using accounting software can streamline this process.

5. Hire and Train Employees

Recruit local talent to support your business operations. Ensure that employment contracts are clear and comply with local labor laws. Investing in employee training can help align them with your business goals and enhance productivity.

6. Establish a Local Presence

Set up your office or physical presence in a suitable location. Consider factors like accessibility, infrastructure, and proximity to your target market. Register your office with local authorities as required.

In conclusion, setting up a business in India involves several structured steps, from choosing the right business structure to ensuring compliance with local regulations. By following this guide, you can navigate the process efficiently and establish a successful presence in the Indian market.

Choosing the Right Location for Your R&D Center

Selecting the perfect location for your R&D center in India is a critical decision that can significantly impact your business's success. India offers a variety of locations, each with unique advantages, catering to different business needs and preferences.

Bangalore: The Silicon Valley of India

Bangalore, often referred to as the Silicon Valley of India, is the top choice for many tech companies looking to establish their R&D centers. The city is renowned for its vibrant tech ecosystem, skilled workforce, and innovative environment.

Advantages:

- Talent Pool: Home to prestigious institutions like the Indian Institute of Science (IISc) and numerous engineering colleges, Bangalore offers a vast pool of highly skilled professionals.
- Tech Ecosystem: The presence of global tech giants and numerous startups creates a collaborative and dynamic environment.
- Infrastructure: Well-developed infrastructure with world-class office spaces, co-working hubs, and reliable connectivity.

When a leading European software company set up its R&D center in Bangalore, it benefited from the city's robust tech ecosystem and access to top-tier talent, accelerating its innovation efforts.

Hyderabad: The Emerging Tech Hub

Hyderabad is rapidly emerging as a preferred destination for tech and R&D activities. Known as "Cyberabad," it offers a conducive environment for technology and innovation.

Advantages:

- Cost-Effective: Compared to Bangalore, Hyderabad offers more affordable real estate and lower operational costs.
- Government Support: The Telangana state government actively supports tech initiatives with policies and incentives.
- Infrastructure: State-of-the-art IT parks like HITEC City provide excellent facilities and connectivity.

A US-based biotech firm chose Hyderabad for its R&D center due to the city's supportive government policies and cost advantages, enabling significant savings and operational efficiency.

Pune: The Educational Hub

Pune, known for its educational institutions, is another attractive location for R&D centers. The city combines a rich talent pool with a pleasant living environment.

Advantages:

- Talent Pool: With numerous universities and technical institutes, Pune offers a steady supply of skilled graduates.
- Quality of Life: The city's relatively lower living costs and pleasant climate make it an attractive location for employees.
- Proximity to Mumbai: Close proximity to Mumbai provides additional business and logistical advantages.

A global automotive company established its R&D center in Pune, leveraging the city's talent and proximity to its manufacturing units in

Maharashtra.

Chennai: The Industrial Powerhouse

Chennai is known for its strong industrial base and is an ideal location for R&D centers focused on manufacturing and automotive sectors.

Advantages:

- Industrial Ecosystem: Chennai's well-established industrial ecosystem supports R&D in manufacturing and engineering.
- Skilled Workforce: Access to skilled labor from premier institutions like IIT Madras.
- Port Access: Chennai's port facilitates easy import and export of goods and equipment.

An international electronics manufacturer chose Chennai for its R&D center, benefiting from the city's robust industrial infrastructure and skilled workforce.

Ahmedabad: The Rising Star

Ahmedabad is known for its strong industrial background and growing educational infrastructure.

Advantages:

- Business-Friendly Environment: Gujarat is known for its pro-business policies and support for industrial growth.
- Educational Institutions: With institutions like the Indian Institute of Management Ahmedabad (IIMA) and numerous engineering colleges, the city offers a talented workforce.
- Cost-Effective: Lower operational costs compared to metros like Bangalore and Mumbai.

Odoo established its R&D center near Ahmedabad, taking advantage of the state policy for operational advantages and talented people to hire.

In conclusion, choosing the right location for your R&D center in India involves considering factors like the talent pool, cost, infrastructure, and specific industry needs. Cities like Bangalore, Hyderabad, Pune, Chennai, and Ahmedabad each offer unique advantages that can support and enhance your business's R&D efforts. By aligning your location choice with your strategic goals, you can leverage India's diverse opportunities to drive innovation and growth.

Overview of India's Infrastructure

A Transformative Journey

India's infrastructure has undergone a remarkable transformation, making it a compelling destination for businesses worldwide. From state-of-the-art highways to cutting-edge digital networks, India's infrastructure supports robust business operations and seamless connectivity.

Transportation Networks

Highways and Roads: India boasts one of the world's largest road networks, spanning over 6.2 million kilometers. The Golden Quadrilateral, a highway network connecting Delhi, Mumbai, Chennai, and Kolkata, exemplifies the modern, high-speed roadways facilitating efficient transport and logistics. Recent projects like Bharatmala Pariyojana aim to further enhance road connectivity, reducing travel time and improving access to remote areas.

Railways: Indian Railways, one of the largest railway networks globally, plays a crucial role in freight and passenger transport. With over 67,000 kilometers of track, it connects nearly every corner of the country. The

Dedicated Freight Corridors (DFCs), such as the Western and Eastern DFCs, are game-changers, significantly increasing the speed and efficiency of cargo movement.

Ports and Airports: India's coastline of 7,500 kilometers is dotted with major ports like Mumbai, Chennai, and Kolkata, handling over 1,400 million tonnes of cargo annually. The Sagarmala project aims to modernize these ports, boosting maritime trade. Additionally, India has over 130 operational airports, with major hubs like Delhi, Mumbai, and Bangalore providing international connectivity. The UDAN scheme enhances regional air connectivity, making travel more accessible across the country.

Digital Infrastructure

Internet Penetration: India is home to the second-largest internet user base globally, with over 700 million users. The Digital India initiative aims to provide high-speed internet access to all citizens, bridging the digital divide and enabling e-governance, e-commerce, and digital payments.

Telecommunication: With a robust telecommunication network, India has over 1.2 billion mobile phone users. The rollout of 5G technology promises to revolutionize connectivity, enabling faster data speeds and supporting the growth of IoT (Internet of Things) and smart cities.

Energy Infrastructure

Power Generation: India is the third-largest producer of electricity globally, with a diverse energy mix including coal, hydro, nuclear, and renewables. The government's focus on renewable energy has led to significant investments in solar and wind power, making India one of the top renewable energy producers.

Smart Grids: India is investing in smart grid technology to improve the efficiency and reliability of electricity distribution. Initiatives like the National Smart Grid Mission aim to modernize the power sector, reducing losses and ensuring a stable power supply.

When a leading US-based manufacturing firm decided to set up a plant in India, they were impressed by the country's advanced infrastructure. The well-connected highways facilitated smooth logistics, while the robust digital infrastructure supported their business operations seamlessly. The availability of reliable power and the push towards renewable energy ensured a sustainable and efficient production process.

India's infrastructure, encompassing transportation, digital networks, and energy systems, provides a solid foundation for business operations. With ongoing investments and modernization efforts, the infrastructure landscape is set to become even more conducive for international businesses. By leveraging these robust facilities, businesses from the USA and Europe can thrive and expand in the Indian market, tapping into the country's vast potential and dynamic economy.

Chapter 4: Building Your Indian Team

Recruiting the Best Talent

Strategies for attracting top talent

Navigating the hiring process

Training and Development

Building a strong training program

Fostering innovation and creativity

Strategies for Attracting Top Talent

Section 1: Understanding the Talent Landscape in India

India boasts a vast talent pool, with over 1.5 million engineering graduates and 200,000 IT professionals entering the workforce each year. Let's explore the practical strategies to attract this top-tier talent. For USA and European business owners, understanding the landscape is crucial. India is home to numerous educational institutions producing highly skilled professionals. Cities like Bengaluru, Hyderabad, Pune, and Ahmedabad are known for their tech-savvy population, making them prime locations for recruitment drives.

Consider the case of ABC Tech, a mid-sized American IT company. They set up their R&D center in Bengaluru and tapped into the local universities by organizing hackathons and workshops. This not only showcased their brand but also helped them identify and recruit top talent who were already familiar with their technology stack.

Advantages:

- Access to a large pool of highly educated professionals.
- Opportunities to engage with talent early through academic partnerships.
- The potential to recruit candidates with specialized skills tailored to your business needs.

Section 2: Building a Strong Employer Brand

One of the key strategies to attract top talent is to establish a strong employer brand. This involves creating a positive image that appeals to potential employees. Business owners from the USA and Europe can achieve this by highlighting their company's culture, growth opportunities, and commitment to innovation.

Leverage social media and professional networks like LinkedIn to share success stories, employee testimonials, and insights into your company's work environment. Engage with potential candidates by offering webinars, virtual tours, and Q&A sessions with your current employees.

Consider the case of XYZ Corp, a European software company, successfully attracted top Indian talent by showcasing their commitment to employee growth and development. They highlighted their flexible working hours, continuous learning opportunities, and a collaborative work culture. This approach resonated with many Indian professionals who value work-life balance and career progression.

Advantages:

- Enhanced visibility and attractiveness of your company to potential candidates.
- Building trust and a positive perception among the talent pool.
- Differentiation from competitors who may not have a strong employer brand presence.

Section 3: Competitive Compensation and Benefits Packages

To attract the best talent, offering competitive compensation and benefits is essential. Indian professionals are not just looking for attractive salaries; they also value comprehensive benefits packages that include health insurance, retirement plans, and opportunities for professional development.

Conduct market research to understand the standard compensation packages within your industry in India. Offer salaries that are not only competitive but also come with additional perks like performance bonuses, stock options, and wellness programs.

An American R&D firm, entered the Indian market by offering compensation packages that were 15% above the industry standard. They also included unique benefits such as international travel opportunities, advanced training programs, and a focus on mental health and well-being. This approach helped them attract top-tier talent who were looking for more than just a paycheck.

Advantages:

- Attraction of high-caliber candidates who are looking for comprehensive rewards.
- Increased retention rates due to attractive and holistic compensation packages.
- Positioning your company as a premium employer in the Indian market.

Attracting top talent in India requires a strategic approach that combines understanding the local talent landscape, building a strong employer brand, and offering competitive compensation packages. By implementing these practical strategies, USA and Europe business owners can tap into India's vast pool of skilled professionals, ensuring their business operations in India are staffed with the best talent available. This not only enhances the quality of work but also contributes to the long-term success and growth of their international ventures.

Navigating the Hiring Process

Section 1: Understanding the Indian Hiring Landscape

Navigating the hiring process in India requires a deep understanding of the local job market, culture, and expectations. India's talent pool is vast and diverse, offering a rich blend of skills and expertise. However, the hiring process can be different from what USA and European business owners are accustomed to.

Familiarize yourself with the various job portals, recruitment agencies, and university placement cells. Naukri, LinkedIn, and Indeed are popular job portals in India. Partnering with reputable recruitment agencies can streamline the hiring process and provide access to a wider talent pool.

An US-based software company. When they decided to set up an R&D center in Pune, they partnered with a local recruitment agency. This agency not only helped them understand the local hiring norms but also provided them with a list of pre-screened candidates, significantly reducing the time and effort involved in the initial stages of recruitment.

Advantages:

- Access to a larger and more diverse pool of candidates.
- Insights into local hiring practices and candidate expectations.
- Reduced time-to-hire through partnerships with local agencies.

Section 2: Crafting an Effective Job Description

A well-crafted job description is crucial for attracting the right candidates. It should be clear, concise, and tailored to the Indian job market. Highlighting the unique aspects of your company and the opportunities for growth can make your job postings stand out.

Ensure that your job descriptions are detailed and specific. Include information about the role, responsibilities, required skills, and career growth opportunities. Emphasize what makes your company a great place to work, such as a collaborative culture, opportunities for international exposure, and a focus on innovation.

An European AI firm, struggled to attract suitable candidates with their generic job descriptions. After revamping their job postings to include details about their cutting-edge projects, flexible work culture, and opportunities for professional development, they saw a significant increase in the quality and quantity of applicants.

Advantages:

- Attracts candidates who are a better fit for the role and the company.
- Reduces the number of irrelevant applications.
- Enhances the company's image as an employer of choice.

Section 3: Streamlining the Interview and Selection Process

The interview and selection process is your opportunity to assess candidates and showcase your company. A structured and transparent process can make a positive impression on candidates and help you make informed hiring decisions.

Implement a multi-stage interview process that includes initial screenings, technical assessments, and cultural fit interviews. Use technology to your advantage by conducting video interviews and utilizing assessment tools. Ensure timely communication with candidates to keep them engaged and informed throughout the process.

An US-based IT services company, adopted a structured interview process when hiring for their new office in Bengaluru. They started with initial phone screenings, followed by technical assessments conducted through an online platform. The final round involved video interviews with team leaders to assess cultural fit. This approach not only streamlined the process but also provided a comprehensive evaluation of each candidate.

Advantages:

- Ensures a thorough evaluation of candidates' skills and fit for the company.
- Enhances the candidate experience through clear and timely communication.
- Reduces the likelihood of hiring mismatches.

Navigating the hiring process in India involves understanding the local job market, crafting effective job descriptions, and streamlining the interview and selection process. By implementing these practical strategies, USA and Europe business owners can effectively attract and hire top talent in India. This not only helps in building a strong and competent team but also contributes to the overall success of their business operations in India. Through real-world examples and best practices, it becomes evident that a strategic approach to hiring can yield significant benefits, ensuring that businesses tap into India's vast talent pool effectively.

Building a Strong Training Program

Section 1: Assessing Training Needs

To build a strong training program, it's essential first to assess the specific needs of your team. Understanding the gaps in skills and knowledge will help in designing a tailored training program that addresses the unique requirements of your business and workforce in India.

Conduct a comprehensive skills assessment through surveys, interviews, and performance reviews. Engage with employees to understand their career aspirations and areas where they seek improvement. Use this data to identify the key competencies and skills that need to be developed.

An European software company, established its first Indian office in Ahmedabad. They conducted a thorough skills assessment and discovered that while their Indian team was highly proficient in technical skills, there was a gap in project management and client communication skills. By identifying these specific needs, they tailored their training program to include workshops on project management and communication skills, ensuring their team could effectively manage international projects.

Advantages:

- Customized training programs that address specific skills gaps.
- Improved employee performance and productivity.
- Enhanced alignment between individual career goals and organizational objectives.

Section 2: Designing a Comprehensive Training Curriculum

Once the training needs are assessed, the next step is to design a comprehensive training curriculum that covers both technical and soft skills. A well-rounded training program ensures that employees are not only proficient in their core job functions but also equipped with the skills needed to thrive in a global business environment.

Develop a curriculum that includes a mix of classroom training, online courses, hands-on workshops, and mentoring programs. Incorporate real-world scenarios and case studies relevant to your industry to make the training more engaging and applicable. Collaborate with local training institutes and universities to leverage their expertise and resources.

An US-based R&D firm, partnered with a local university in Bengaluru to create a specialized training program. This program included modules on the latest technological advancements, cross-cultural communication, and leadership development. By offering a diverse range of training formats and collaborating with educational institutions, the company ensured its employees received high-quality training tailored to their needs.

Advantages:

- Comprehensive skill development covering both technical and soft skills.
- Increased employee engagement through diverse and interactive training methods.
- Access to specialized knowledge and resources through partnerships with local institutions.

Section 3: Implementing and Monitoring the Training Program

Effective implementation and continuous monitoring are crucial to the success of any training program. Regular feedback and assessment help in fine-tuning the training process and ensuring that it meets the evolving needs of the organization and its employees.

Establish clear objectives and key performance indicators (KPIs) for the training program. Use learning management systems (LMS) to track progress and performance. Regularly collect feedback from participants and trainers to identify areas of improvement. Conduct periodic assessments to measure the effectiveness of the training and make necessary adjustments.

An American IT services company, implemented a robust LMS to manage their training program in India. They set clear KPIs such as increased project delivery efficiency and improved client satisfaction scores. By continuously monitoring progress and incorporating feedback, they were able to adapt their training modules to better suit the needs of their employees, resulting in significant performance improvements.

Advantages:

- Clear tracking of training progress and effectiveness.
- Continuous improvement through regular feedback and assessments.
- Enhanced alignment of training outcomes with business goals.

Building a strong training program in India involves assessing training needs, designing a comprehensive curriculum, and effectively implementing and monitoring the program. By following these practical strategies, USA and European business owners can ensure their Indian teams are well-equipped with the necessary skills to excel in a global business environment. Through real-world examples and best practices, it becomes evident that a strategic approach to training and development can lead to significant benefits, including improved employee performance, higher engagement, and better alignment with organizational goals.

Fostering Innovation and Creativity

Section 1: Creating a Culture of Innovation

Creating a culture that encourages innovation and creativity is essential for any business aiming to thrive in today's competitive landscape. For USA and European business owners setting up in India, this involves understanding the local work environment and integrating global best practices.

Encourage open communication and collaboration among team members. Implement regular brainstorming sessions and innovation workshops where employees feel safe to share their ideas without fear of criticism. Foster a supportive environment that rewards creativity and innovative thinking.

An US-based tech company that expanded to Mumbai. They introduced "Innovation Fridays," where employees could work on any project they were passionate about. This initiative not only boosted creativity but also led to several breakthrough ideas that were later implemented in their core business.

Advantages:

- Encourages a continuous flow of fresh ideas and perspectives.
- Enhances employee engagement and job satisfaction.
- Drives business growth through innovative solutions and products.

Section 2: Leveraging Diverse Talent

India's diverse talent pool is a significant asset for fostering innovation. Tapping into this diversity can lead to unique solutions and creative problem-solving. Embracing different cultural perspectives and backgrounds enriches the ideation process.

Build diverse teams that include members from various regions, backgrounds, and expertise. Encourage cross-functional collaboration to bring different viewpoints into the innovation process. Provide diversity training to ensure an inclusive environment where all voices are heard and valued.

An European manufacturing firm, set up an innovation lab in Bengaluru. They recruited a diverse team of engineers, designers, and market analysts from different parts of India. This diversity in thought and experience led to the development of a new product line that was highly successful in both domestic and international markets.

Advantages:

- Brings together a wide range of ideas and perspectives.

- Promotes creative problem-solving and innovation.
- Enhances the company's ability to cater to diverse markets and customers.

Section 3: Implementing Continuous Learning and Development

Continuous learning is vital for maintaining a culture of innovation. Providing employees with opportunities to learn new skills and stay updated with industry trends keeps the creative juices flowing and ensures that your team is equipped to tackle future challenges.

Offer regular training programs, workshops, and access to online courses. Encourage employees to attend industry conferences and seminars. Implement a mentorship program where experienced professionals can guide and inspire newer employees.

An American R&D firm, partnered with a leading Indian university to offer advanced courses in emerging technologies. They also encouraged their employees to participate in international tech conferences. This commitment to continuous learning not only kept their team at the forefront of technological advancements but also sparked numerous innovative projects within the company.

Advantages:

- Ensures employees have the latest skills and knowledge.
- Keeps the team motivated and engaged.
- Encourages the adoption of new technologies and innovative practices.

Fostering innovation and creativity within your Indian team involves creating a culture of open communication, leveraging diverse talent, and implementing continuous learning and development programs. By following these practical strategies, USA and European business owners can harness the full potential of India's vibrant talent pool, driving growth and innovation in their business operations. Through real-world examples and best practices, it becomes evident that a strategic approach to fostering innovation can lead to significant advantages, including enhanced employee engagement, unique solutions, and sustained business success.

Chapter 5: Ensuring Control and Transparency

Managing Your Indian Operations

Best practices for management and oversight

Tools and technologies for transparency

Maintaining Quality and Standards

Ensuring high-quality output

Managing Your Indian Operations

Best Practices for Management and Oversight

Partner with Local Companies

One of the first steps in managing operations in India is to partner with reputable local companies. This approach helps in understanding the local market, navigating bureaucratic hurdles, and accessing established networks. For example, a US-based tech firm partnered with an Indian IT service provider to leverage their local expertise and resources, ensuring a smoother entry into the market.

Hire Experienced Local Managers

Finding and hiring managers with experience in handling Indian operations is crucial. These individuals understand the nuances of the local business environment and can bridge the cultural and operational gaps between the parent company and the Indian branch. A European manufacturing firm, for instance, successfully scaled their operations in India by hiring a local CEO with extensive industry experience.

Start Small and Scale Up

Begin with a smaller, manageable project to test the waters. This allows for better risk management and gradual acclimatization to the Indian business landscape. An US healthcare company initially launched a pilot project in India, which, after successful implementation, expanded into a full-scale operation.

Understand Local Regulations

Compliance with Indian laws and regulations is non-negotiable. Engaging with local legal advisors to ensure all operations are above board is essential.

An American finance firm faced significant challenges due to regulatory misunderstandings but overcame them by consulting with Indian legal experts.

Cultural Sensitivity Training

Providing cultural sensitivity training for your management team can enhance communication and reduce misunderstandings. This practice was instrumental for a European retail giant, whose managers underwent extensive training to better integrate with their Indian counterparts.

Regular Communication Channels

Establishing regular communication channels ensures transparency and timely updates. Weekly video calls, monthly reports, and quarterly reviews can keep everyone aligned. A US-based software company set up a robust communication schedule with their Indian team, which led to better project management and fewer delays.

Integrated IT Systems

Utilizing integrated IT systems for real-time monitoring and management can enhance oversight. Cloud-based project management tools and collaborative platforms allow for seamless coordination. For instance, a European engineering firm adopted a comprehensive ERP system to monitor their Indian operations, significantly improving efficiency.

On-site Visits

Regular visits by senior management to the Indian operations can foster better relationships and provide a firsthand understanding of the ground realities. A US-based consulting firm's leadership team made biannual visits to their Indian offices, strengthening trust and collaboration.

Performance Metrics and KPIs

Defining clear performance metrics and key performance indicators (KPIs) helps in monitoring progress and achieving business goals. An American logistics company implemented a detailed KPI framework for their Indian branch, leading to enhanced accountability and performance.

Feedback Mechanisms

Implementing robust feedback mechanisms allows for continuous improvement. Encouraging open dialogue and promptly addressing issues can significantly improve operations. A European pharmaceutical company's feedback system in India helped identify and resolve operational bottlenecks swiftly.

Empower Local Teams

Empowering your local teams by giving them decision-making authority can lead to more responsive and agile operations. A US tech startup empowered their Indian R&D team to make critical project decisions, resulting in faster innovation cycles.

Invest in Training and Development

Investing in the continuous development of your Indian workforce ensures they stay updated with the latest industry trends and technologies. A European automotive company's extensive training programs in India enhanced their employees' skills and productivity.

Transparent Governance

Implementing transparent governance practices builds trust and accountability. Regular audits and clear reporting structures are essential. An American consumer goods company's transparent governance model in India led to improved compliance and operational integrity.

Local Community Engagement

Engaging with the local community can enhance your company's reputation and create a positive work environment. A European food processing company's community outreach programs in India fostered goodwill and local support.

Adaptability and Flexibility

The ability to adapt to local conditions and remain flexible in your approach is vital. A US-based fashion retailer's flexibility in adapting their product line to suit Indian tastes helped them gain a competitive edge.

By incorporating these best practices, USA and European business owners can effectively manage their Indian operations, ensuring control, transparency, and sustained success. Real-world examples highlight the importance of these strategies in navigating the complexities of the Indian market, ultimately leading to thriving business ventures.

Tools and Technologies for Transparency

Microsoft Teams: Offers seamless video conferencing, chat, and file sharing, ensuring all team members stay connected and informed in real-time. Ideal for bridging the distance between US, European, and Indian teams.

Slack: A powerful messaging app that integrates with various other tools, promoting efficient communication and collaboration across different time zones. It helps streamline project discussions and updates.

Asana: Provides a user-friendly interface for task assignment, tracking, and project timelines, enhancing visibility and accountability across all levels of the organization.

Trello: Utilizes a visual board and card system to manage projects, making it easy to monitor progress and ensure that everyone is aligned on priorities and deadlines.

Jira: Specifically designed for software development teams, offering robust issue and project tracking capabilities. It helps manage complex projects with detailed workflows and reporting.

Monday.com: An intuitive project management tool that allows customization of workflows and integration with other software, facilitating better project oversight and management.

Google Analytics: Provides insights into website and app performance, allowing businesses to track user engagement and make data-driven decisions for their Indian operations.

Odoo: An all-in-one business software that offers a suite of integrated applications, including CRM, ERP, and project management, ensuring comprehensive oversight and streamlined operations.

Zoho Analytics: Offers advanced analytics and reporting features that help monitor various business metrics, ensuring transparency and informed decision-making.

Power BI: Microsoft's powerful analytics service that integrates with multiple data sources, providing comprehensive reports and dashboards for better operational transparency.

By leveraging these tools, USA and European business owners can ensure effective management, enhanced communication, and clear visibility into their Indian operations, leading to improved control and transparency. Real-world examples of these tools in action highlight their utility in maintaining smooth and efficient cross-border operations.

Maintaining Quality and Standards

Ensuring High-Quality Output

Establishing Robust Quality Control Processes

Define Clear Quality Standards: Begin by establishing clear, measurable quality standards that align with global best practices. This helps ensure that everyone involved in the production process understands the benchmarks they need to meet. For instance, a US-based electronics company defined stringent quality metrics for their Indian manufacturing unit, resulting in consistent high-quality outputs.

Implement Standard Operating Procedures (SOPs): Developing and strictly adhering to SOPs can minimize variability and ensure uniformity in processes. An example is a European pharmaceutical company that introduced detailed SOPs for their Indian subsidiary, which significantly reduced defects and improved product consistency.

Regular Audits and Inspections: Conducting regular internal and external audits helps in identifying deviations from quality standards and implementing corrective actions promptly. A real-world case is an American textile firm that scheduled quarterly audits for its Indian operations, ensuring compliance and continuous improvement.

Invest in Advanced Quality Management Systems (QMS): Leveraging advanced QMS software can streamline quality control processes, track performance, and ensure compliance with industry standards. For example, a European automotive parts manufacturer implemented a sophisticated QMS in their Indian plant, leading to enhanced quality assurance and regulatory compliance.

Training and Development

Continuous Training Programs: Regular training programs for employees ensure they are up-to-date with the latest quality control techniques and standards. A US software company's continuous training initiatives for their Indian developers led to higher code quality and fewer post-release bugs.

Skill Development Workshops: Conducting skill development workshops can enhance the technical capabilities of the workforce, leading to better quality output. A European engineering firm's investment in skill workshops for their Indian team resulted in more precise and reliable product designs.

Cross-functional Training: Encouraging cross-functional training can improve employees' understanding of the entire production process, fostering better quality control. For instance, a US-based consumer goods company's cross-functional training programs in India improved coordination and overall product quality.

Leveraging Technology and Innovation

Adopt Automation and AI: Integrating automation and AI into the production process can significantly enhance precision and reduce human errors. An American electronics company's use of AI-driven quality checks in their Indian facility led to a substantial reduction in defects.

Utilize Data Analytics: Data analytics tools can provide insights into quality trends and potential issues, allowing for proactive quality management. A European logistics company used data analytics to monitor their Indian operations, identifying and addressing quality issues before they escalated.

Encourage Innovation: Fostering a culture of innovation among employees can lead to creative solutions for maintaining high quality. A US-based healthcare company's innovation-driven approach in their Indian R&D center resulted in breakthrough quality improvements in their medical devices.

By implementing these best practices, USA and European business owners can ensure high-quality outputs from their Indian operations. Real-world examples demonstrate how robust quality control processes, continuous training, and leveraging technology can lead to superior quality and competitive advantage in the global market.

Chapter 6: Beyond Outsourcing

The Downside of Traditional Outsourcing

Common pitfalls of outsourcing

Why establishing your own operations is better

Case Studies: Success Stories

Real-world examples of businesses thriving with in-house operations

Common Pitfalls of Outsourcing

Outsourcing has long been a strategy for businesses aiming to reduce costs, access specialized skills, and increase efficiency. While it offers several advantages, it also comes with significant challenges. In this subchapter, we'll explore the standard outsourcing process, its benefits, and the common pitfalls that business owners should be aware of.

Understanding the Standard Outsourcing Process

1. Identifying Needs and Selecting a Vendor

The outsourcing process typically begins with identifying the business functions or processes that can be outsourced. Companies assess their needs and search for vendors who specialize in those areas. This involves a thorough evaluation of potential vendors' capabilities, track record, and financial stability. For example, a US-based tech company looking to outsource its customer support might shortlist vendors from countries known for their English proficiency and customer service expertise.

2. Contract Negotiation and Agreement

Once a vendor is selected, the next step is negotiating the terms of the contract. This includes defining the scope of work, service level agreements (SLAs), pricing models, confidentiality clauses, and other legal and operational aspects. An example would be a European pharmaceutical company drafting a contract with an Indian IT firm to handle their software development needs, outlining specific milestones and quality benchmarks.

3. Transition and Knowledge Transfer

The transition phase involves transferring knowledge and processes from the client to the vendor. This step is critical to ensure that the vendor fully understands the client's business processes, goals, and expectations. A practical example is a US financial services firm conducting detailed training sessions with their new outsourcing partner to ensure seamless knowledge transfer.

4. Ongoing Management and Monitoring

After the initial setup, ongoing management and monitoring are essential to maintain quality and ensure the vendor meets performance expectations. Regular communication, performance reviews, and audits are common practices. For instance, a European retail company might schedule monthly meetings with their outsourced marketing team to review progress and address any issues.

Advantages of Outsourcing

1. Cost Reduction

One of the primary advantages of outsourcing is cost savings. Companies can save on labor costs, infrastructure, and other operational expenses by outsourcing to countries with lower cost structures. For example, a US software company outsourcing development to India can benefit from lower wage rates while maintaining high-quality output.

2. Access to Specialized Skills

Outsourcing provides access to a global talent pool, allowing companies to leverage specialized skills that may not be available in-house. A European healthcare firm outsourcing its IT needs to a specialized firm in India gains access to cutting-edge technology and expertise.

3. Increased Efficiency and Focus

By outsourcing non-core functions, businesses can focus on their core competencies and strategic initiatives. This leads to increased efficiency and productivity. For instance, a US-based e-commerce company outsourcing its logistics operations can concentrate on marketing and product development.

Common Pitfalls of Outsourcing

1. Loss of Control

One of the most significant drawbacks of outsourcing is the potential loss of control over business processes. When a third party handles critical functions, it can be challenging to maintain the same level of oversight and control. For example, a European fashion brand faced quality issues when they outsourced production to a low-cost manufacturer, leading to customer dissatisfaction and brand damage.

2. Communication Barriers

Outsourcing often involves working with teams in different countries, leading to communication challenges due to time zone differences, language barriers, and cultural differences. A US-based tech firm experienced delays and misunderstandings when outsourcing to a vendor in a different time zone, impacting project timelines.

3. Hidden Costs

While outsourcing promises cost savings, hidden costs can erode these benefits. These may include expenses related to vendor selection, contract negotiation, transition, ongoing management, and potential rework due to quality issues. For instance, a European financial services company underestimated the costs of managing an outsourced IT project, leading to budget overruns.

4. Quality and Consistency Issues

Maintaining consistent quality can be difficult when outsourcing, especially if the vendor's standards do not match those of the client. A US healthcare company encountered quality issues when their outsourced medical billing service provider did not adhere to stringent regulatory standards, leading to compliance problems.

5. Dependency on the Vendor

Over-reliance on an outsourcing partner can create risks, especially if the vendor faces financial difficulties or fails to deliver. For example, a European automotive company had to halt production temporarily when their sole outsourced supplier faced bankruptcy.

6. Security and Confidentiality Risks

Outsourcing involves sharing sensitive business information with a third party, increasing the risk of data breaches and intellectual property theft. A US-based legal firm faced a data breach when their outsourced IT service provider failed to implement adequate security measures.

7. Cultural Misalignment

Cultural differences can lead to misunderstandings and misaligned expectations. For instance, a European marketing firm outsourcing to an Indian agency struggled with different working styles and business practices, affecting collaboration and results.

8. Legal and Compliance Issues

Navigating legal and regulatory requirements across different countries can be complex and challenging. A US pharmaceutical company faced legal challenges when their outsourced manufacturing partner in Asia did not comply with local regulations.

9. Reduced Employee Morale

Outsourcing can negatively impact the morale of existing employees, who may fear job losses or reduced responsibilities. A European bank experienced lower employee morale and productivity after outsourcing their customer service department.

10. Long-term Sustainability

Finally, while outsourcing may offer short-term gains, it can sometimes compromise long-term sustainability and innovation. Companies that rely heavily on outsourcing may miss out on developing in-house expertise and capabilities. For example, a US tech startup realized the limitations of their outsourced development model when they needed to innovate rapidly to stay competitive.

By understanding these common pitfalls, USA and European business owners can make informed decisions about outsourcing and explore alternative strategies that offer greater control, quality, and long-term success.

Why Establishing Your Own Operations in India is Better

Outsourcing has been a common strategy for many Western businesses seeking cost savings and specialized skills. However, as companies grow and aim for more control and higher standards, establishing their own operations in India proves to be a superior strategy. This subchapter explores why setting up your own operations in India can offer substantial benefits, illustrated with real-world examples and best practices.

The Need for Greater Control and Oversight

Full Control Over Processes

By setting up your own operations, you maintain complete control over business processes. This control ensures that your quality standards and operational procedures are consistently met without relying on third-party vendors. For instance, when a US-based electronics company established its manufacturing unit in India, it resulted in higher quality products and greater customer satisfaction because the company could enforce its stringent quality standards directly.

Enhanced Communication

Managing your own team in India eliminates many of the communication barriers associated with outsourcing. With direct oversight and regular face-to-face interactions, either in person or via video conferencing, you can ensure clearer communication and faster decision-making. A European software company saw significant improvements in project timelines and outcomes after setting up a dedicated office in Ahmedabad, where direct interaction fostered better understanding and quicker resolutions.

Predictable Costs and Investments

While the initial setup costs for establishing your own operations may be higher, this approach can be more cost-effective in the long run. You avoid the hidden costs associated with outsourcing, such as vendor management, transition expenses, and quality control issues. A US healthcare firm discovered that owning their Indian facilities led to lower long-term costs and better financial planning, providing a clearer picture of future investments.

Consistency, Quality, and Innovation

Consistent Quality and Standards

By training your own staff and implementing your quality control systems, you can ensure that your products and services consistently meet your standards. A European automotive parts manufacturer established a plant in Pune, leading to consistently high-quality outputs and reduced defect rates. The ability to monitor and tweak processes in real-time helped maintain these high standards.

Building a Strong Company Culture

Having your own operations allows you to instill your company's values and culture directly into your workforce. This alignment fosters loyalty, higher employee engagement, and a shared vision. A US tech giant built a vibrant and innovative work culture in their Indian R&D center, leading to high retention rates and groundbreaking innovations, as employees felt more connected to the company's mission.

Intellectual Property Security

Managing your own operations significantly reduces the risk of data breaches and intellectual property theft, as you can implement and enforce stringent security measures. A US-based legal firm benefited from enhanced data security after establishing its own IT support center in India, where they could closely monitor and protect sensitive information.

Flexibility and Agility

Having your own operations in India allows for greater flexibility and agility in responding to market changes and opportunities. A European fashion retailer swiftly adapted to local trends and preferences by managing its own production facility in India, enabling them to quickly adjust their offerings based on real-time market feedback.

Strategic Advantages and Market Insights

Long-term Strategic Benefits

Establishing your own operations can provide long-term strategic advantages, such as developing local expertise, fostering innovation, and creating a sustainable competitive edge. A US-based consumer electronics company leveraged its Indian R&D center to drive innovation and maintain a competitive edge in the global market, as the direct control over research and development led to faster innovation cycles.

Local Market Insights

Having a direct presence in India enables you to gain deeper insights into the local market, consumer behavior, and emerging trends. This knowledge can inform your overall business strategy. A European FMCG company used insights from its Indian operations to successfully launch new products tailored to local preferences, significantly increasing their market share.

Enhanced Collaboration and Synergy

Directly managing your operations fosters better collaboration and synergy between your global teams. This integrated approach enhances efficiency and drives better overall business performance. A US-based pharmaceutical company experienced improved collaboration between its US headquarters and Indian research center, leading to faster drug development cycles.

Talent Development and Retention

Having your own operations allows for better talent development and retention. You can invest in your employees' growth, which in turn increases their loyalty and productivity. A US tech firm that set up operations in India offered continuous training and development programs, resulting in a highly skilled and dedicated workforce.

Brand and Reputation Management

Managing your operations helps protect and enhance your brand reputation. A European luxury goods company found that having their own retail stores in India allowed them to control the customer experience better and maintain their brand's premium image.

Establishing your own operations in India presents numerous benefits over traditional outsourcing. From greater control and consistent quality to enhanced communication and strategic advantages, this approach allows businesses to leverage India's vast talent pool and growing infrastructure more effectively.

By understanding and implementing these practices, USA and European business owners can make informed decisions that align with their strategic goals, ensuring their operations in India not only thrive but also drive global success.

A Success Story of Odoo thriving with in-house operations in India

Odoo, a leading provider of open-source business applications, serves as an exemplary case of how establishing operations in India can yield significant benefits. This success story illustrates the advantages of direct investment and highlights best practices for USA and European business owners considering a similar move.

The Decision to Establish Operations in India

Odoo, headquartered in Belgium, recognized the potential of India's vast talent pool and growing market. The company decided to set up its own operations in India rather than outsourcing, aiming to achieve greater control over its processes and leverage local expertise directly.

Identifying Opportunities

Odoo saw India as a strategic location due to its large pool of skilled IT professionals and a burgeoning market for enterprise software. The company anticipated that a local presence would enable it to tap into these resources more effectively than through outsourcing.

Initial Setup and Investment

Odoo invested in a state-of-the-art office in Gandhinagar, Gujarat, strategically located to attract top talent from nearby educational hubs. The initial setup included hiring local managers with extensive experience in the Indian market, ensuring a smooth transition and effective operations.

Implementation and Growth

Building a Strong Team

Odoo's primary focus was on building a strong, dedicated team. They conducted rigorous recruitment drives at local universities and offered competitive salaries and growth opportunities to attract the best talent. This approach resulted in a team of highly skilled developers, engineers, and support staff who were well-versed in Odoo's technology and business model.

Training and Development

Odoo emphasized continuous training and development, ensuring that their Indian employees were always at the forefront of technological advancements. Regular workshops, training sessions, and cross-functional projects helped in maintaining high standards of quality and innovation. This focus on development created a loyal and motivated workforce, contributing significantly to Odoo's success.

Quality Control and Standards

By having their own operations, Odoo could implement stringent quality control measures. They developed detailed Standard Operating Procedures (SOPs) and conducted regular audits to ensure compliance with international standards. This hands-on approach helped in maintaining consistency and high quality in their products and services.

Achieving Success and Strategic Advantages

Market Adaptation and Expansion

With a direct presence in India, Odoo was able to adapt its products to better suit the local market. They gathered insights from Indian customers and tailored their offerings to meet specific needs, resulting in a significant increase in market share. Odoo's ERP solutions became particularly popular among small and medium-sized enterprises (SMEs) in India, who benefited from the customizable and cost-effective software.

Innovation and Collaboration

Odoo's Indian operations became a hub for innovation. The close collaboration between the Indian R&D team and the global headquarters led to the development of new features and enhancements that benefited customers worldwide. This synergy fostered a culture of continuous improvement and rapid innovation.

Cost Efficiency and Predictability

While the initial investment was substantial, Odoo found that operating their own facilities in India was more cost-efficient in the long run. They avoided the hidden costs associated with outsourcing and achieved better financial predictability. This stability allowed for more strategic planning and resource allocation.

Enhanced Customer Support

Having a dedicated team in India improved Odoo's customer support capabilities. They could offer 24/7 support to their global clientele, leveraging the time zone differences to ensure continuous service. This enhanced support was a critical factor in increasing customer satisfaction and loyalty.

Building a Strong Brand Presence

Odoo's direct investment in India also helped in building a strong brand presence. They engaged with the local community through corporate social responsibility (CSR) initiatives and participated in industry events and conferences. These efforts not only enhanced their reputation but also established them as a key player in the Indian market.

Conclusion

Odoo's success story in India exemplifies the numerous benefits of establishing direct operations rather than relying on outsourcing. By maintaining control over their processes, fostering a culture of innovation, and leveraging local talent, Odoo has achieved significant growth and market presence. Their experience serves as a valuable lesson for USA and European business owners looking to expand into India.

By understanding the strategic advantages and implementing best practices, businesses can navigate the complexities of the Indian market and unlock its vast potential. Odoo's journey highlights the importance of direct investment in achieving long-term success and maintaining a competitive edge in the global market.

Chapter 7: Comprehensive Support for Your Journey

End-to-End Services

Overview of required services for setting up business in India

How to choose the right service provider

Overcoming Challenges

Common challenges and solutions

Support networks and resources

End-to-End Services

Overview of required services for setting up business in India

1. Market Research: Understand local market dynamics, customer preferences, and competition to inform strategic decisions.
2. Feasibility Studies: Assess the viability of your business idea in the Indian context, considering economic, technical, and legal factors.
3. Business Registration: Navigate the process of registering your business entity in India, ensuring compliance with local regulations.
4. Legal Advisory Services:Obtain expert guidance on Indian laws and regulations to avoid legal pitfalls and ensure smooth operations.
5. Compliance Management: Stay compliant with Indian regulatory requirements, avoiding penalties and ensuring ethical business practices.
6. Taxation Advisory: Receive advice on tax planning, compliance, and optimization to maximize financial efficiency.
7. Accounting Services: Maintain accurate financial records and reports, ensuring transparency and aiding in decision-making.
8. Financial Planning: Develop robust financial strategies to support business growth and stability in the Indian market.
9. Banking Services: Access banking solutions tailored to your business needs, from account management to financing options.
10. Investment Consulting: Get advice on investment opportunities and strategies to grow your business in India.
11. Real Estate Advisory: Find the right property for your business operations, considering location, cost, and future growth.
12. Office Space Leasing: Secure office space that meets your needs in terms of size, location, and budget.

13. R&D Center Setup: Establish a research and development center to innovate and stay competitive in the market.
14. Infrastructure Development: Develop necessary infrastructure to support your business operations, from facilities to utilities.
15. IT Infrastructure Setup: Implement robust IT systems to ensure smooth and secure business operations.
16. Cybersecurity Services: Protect your business from cyber threats with comprehensive cybersecurity solutions.
17. Digital Marketing: Promote your business online to reach a wider audience and drive growth.
18. Branding Services: Create a strong brand identity that resonates with your target market.
19. Website Development: Develop a professional website that showcases your business and facilitates customer interaction.
20. E-commerce Solutions: Set up an e-commerce platform to sell your products or services online.
21. Social Media Management: Engage with your audience and build your brand presence on social media platforms.
22. Public Relations: Manage your company's public image and communicate effectively with stakeholders.
23. HR Consultancy: Develop effective human resource strategies to attract, retain, and manage talent.
24. Recruitment Services: Find the best talent for your business, from entry-level positions to executive roles.
25. Employee Training: Provide training programs to upskill your workforce and enhance productivity.
26. Leadership Development: Cultivate leadership skills within your organization to drive business success.
27. Payroll Management: Ensure accurate and timely payroll processing for your employees.
28. Employee Benefits Administration: Manage employee benefits programs to attract and retain top talent.
29. Immigration Assistance: Navigate the immigration process for expat employees relocating to India.
30. Relocation Services: Facilitate smooth relocation for your employees, from housing to settling in.
31. Cultural Training: Understand Indian cultural nuances to foster better workplace relationships and collaboration.

32. Business Process Outsourcing: Outsource non-core business processes to specialized service providers.
33. Supply Chain Management: Optimize your supply chain for efficiency, cost-effectiveness, and reliability.
34. Logistics Services: Manage the transportation and storage of goods to ensure timely delivery.
35. Inventory Management: Keep track of your inventory to avoid stockouts and overstocking.
36. Customs Clearance: Facilitate the smooth import and export of goods through customs.
37. Import/Export Consulting: Get expert advice on navigating international trade regulations and practices.
38. Quality Control Services: Ensure your products meet quality standards through rigorous testing and inspection.
39. Vendor Management: Effectively manage relationships with suppliers and service providers.
40. Procurement Services: Source goods and services at competitive prices while ensuring quality.
41. Contract Manufacturing: Partner with manufacturers to produce your goods efficiently and cost-effectively.
42. Facility Management: Maintain and manage your business facilities for optimal operation.
43. Office Administration: Handle day-to-day administrative tasks to keep your office running smoothly.
44. Secretarial Services: Manage company records, meetings, and compliance requirements efficiently.
45. Travel and Accommodation Management: Arrange travel and accommodation for business trips and relocating employees.
46. Event Management: Plan and execute business events, from conferences to product launches.
47. Translation Services: Translate documents and communications to bridge language barriers.
48. Interpretation Services: Provide interpretation services for meetings and conferences to ensure clear communication.
49. IT Support Services: Offer technical support to resolve IT issues and maintain system uptime.
50. Software Development: Develop custom software solutions to meet your specific business needs.

51. Application Maintenance: Ensure your software applications run smoothly with regular maintenance and updates.
52. Data Analytics: Leverage data to gain insights and make informed business decisions.
53. Cloud Computing Services: Adopt cloud solutions to enhance scalability, security, and collaboration.
54. ERP Implementation: Integrate enterprise resource planning systems to streamline business processes.
55. CRM Solutions: Implement customer relationship management systems to enhance customer interactions.
56. Customer Support Services: Provide excellent customer service to enhance satisfaction and loyalty.
57. Call Center Services: Set up call centers to handle customer inquiries and support efficiently.
58. Market Entry Strategy Consulting: Develop strategies to successfully enter and thrive in the Indian market.
59. Risk Management: Identify and mitigate risks to protect your business interests.
60. Business Continuity Planning: Ensure your business can continue operating during disruptions with effective planning.
61. Security Services: Protect your business premises and assets with professional security solutions.
62. Insurance Services: Secure the right insurance coverage to protect against potential losses.
63. Government Liaison Services: Navigate interactions with government bodies for permits, licenses, and compliance.
64. Environmental Consulting: Ensure your business adheres to environmental regulations and practices sustainability.
65. Corporate Social Responsibility Consulting: Develop CSR programs that contribute positively to the community and enhance your brand.
66. Intellectual Property Rights Management: Protect your intellectual property through registration and enforcement.
67. Research and Development Services: Drive innovation with dedicated R&D services to stay ahead in the market.
68. Product Development Consulting: Bring new products to market with expert guidance on development processes.
69. Innovation Management: Foster a culture of innovation within your organization to drive growth.

70. Technology Transfer Services: Facilitate the transfer of technology and expertise to enhance your operations.
71. Energy Management: Optimize energy usage to reduce costs and promote sustainability.
72. Waste Management: Implement effective waste management practices to minimize environmental impact.
73. Renewable Energy Solutions: Adopt renewable energy sources to power your business sustainably.
74. Health and Safety Consulting: Ensure workplace safety and compliance with health and safety regulations.
75. Crisis Management: Develop plans to handle emergencies and minimize business disruptions.
76. Investor Relations: Manage relationships with investors and communicate your business performance effectively.
77. Funding and Capital Raising: Secure funding and capital to support your business growth and expansion.
78. Mergers and Acquisitions Advisory: Get expert advice on mergers, acquisitions, and strategic partnerships.
79. Joint Venture Consulting: Explore joint venture opportunities to expand your business capabilities.
80. Partnership Development: Develop strategic partnerships to enhance your business reach and resources.
81. Strategic Planning: Create long-term strategic plans to guide your business towards success.
82. Performance Improvement Consulting: Identify areas for improvement and implement strategies to boost performance.
83. Market Expansion Strategy: Plan and execute strategies to expand your business into new markets.
84. Sales Strategy Development: Develop effective sales strategies to drive revenue and market share.
85. Pricing Strategy Consulting: Determine optimal pricing strategies to maximize profitability.
86. Distribution Network Development: Build efficient distribution networks to ensure product availability.
87. Retail Consulting: Optimize your retail operations for better customer experience and profitability.
88. Franchise Development: Expand your business through franchising opportunities.

89. Customer Experience Consulting: Enhance customer experience to build loyalty and drive repeat business.
90. Loyalty Program Development: Create loyalty programs to reward and retain your best customers.
91. Product Sourcing: Source high-quality products to meet your business needs.
92. Prototyping Services: Develop prototypes to test and refine your products before market launch.
93. Patent Filing Services: Protect your inventions with patent filing and management services.
94. Trademark Registration: Register and protect your brand identity with trademark services.
95. Compliance Audits: Ensure your business operations comply with regulatory standards through audits.
96. Financial Audits: Conduct financial audits to ensure accuracy and transparency in financial reporting.
97. Operational Audits: Review business operations to identify inefficiencies and areas for improvement.
98. Marketing Audits: Evaluate your marketing strategies to enhance effectiveness and ROI.
99. Supply Chain Audits: Assess your supply chain for efficiency and reliability.
100. Sustainability Audits: Ensure your business practices are sustainable and environmentally friendly.
101. Benchmarking Services: Compare your business performance against industry standards and competitors.
102. Competitor Analysis: Analyze competitors to understand their strategies and identify opportunities.
103. Industry Analysis: Gain insights into industry trends and dynamics to inform strategic decisions.
104. Feasibility Analysis: Assess the feasibility of new projects or ventures in the Indian market.
105. Market Intelligence: Gather and analyze market data to make informed business decisions.
106. Business Intelligence: Use business intelligence tools to analyze data and gain strategic insights.
107. Strategic Alliances Consulting: Form strategic alliances to enhance business capabilities and reach.

108. Digital Transformation Consulting: Embrace digital transformation to stay competitive in the modern business landscape.
109. Agile Transformation Services: Adopt agile methodologies to enhance flexibility and responsiveness.
110. Change Management Consulting: Manage organizational change effectively to ensure smooth transitions.

From the above list, multiple services are essential for establishing, operating, and growing your business in India. While some services may not be relevant to your specific business, they are crucial for others. Overall, it is vital to ensure you have the right vendor for each service. Imagine the convenience and efficiency if one company could provide all these services, becoming the bridge that seamlessly facilitates your business's entry and growth in India.

How to Choose the Right Service Provider

In the complex journey of establishing and growing your business in India, choosing the right service provider can be a game-changer. Imagine the sheer convenience and efficiency of working with a single partner who can handle all your needs, from market research to employee training. This approach not only saves you valuable time but also ensures that every aspect of your business setup and operation is seamlessly integrated.

The Benefit of Convenience

Consider the case of a European tech company, which decided to expand its operations to India. Initially, they tried to manage everything independently, from legal registrations to office leasing. They quickly found themselves overwhelmed by the myriad of tasks and the complexity of Indian regulations. After partnering with an end-to-end service provider, they was able to streamline the entire process. The provider handled everything, allowing them to focus on their core business. Within months, they had a fully operational office in Ahmedabad, complete with a talented team and a robust IT infrastructure.

Time-Saving Strategy

By working with a single, comprehensive service provider, you can expedite your business setup in India. Instead of spending months, or even years, navigating the complexities of a new market, your business can be up and running in a matter of weeks. This time-saving strategy is particularly valuable for companies looking to capitalize on the fast-paced opportunities in India's burgeoning market.

Take, for instance, a U.S.-based consumer goods company. They faced stiff competition and needed to enter the Indian market quickly to gain a competitive tech operational edge. Partnering with an all-in-one service provider, they was able to set up their IT operation, establish a team, and launch a global support within a few months. This rapid setup not only saved time but also allowed them to serve their clients better before their competitors could react.

Ensuring Independence for the Future

A competent service provider will not only support you through the initial setup but also equip you with the knowledge and tools to become independent in the long run. They act as a mentor, guiding you through the intricacies of the Indian market and helping you build a self-sustaining operation.

For example, TechVision, a European software company, partnered with a comprehensive service provider to establish their R&D center in Pune. Over time, the service provider trained TechVision's local team to handle various operational aspects independently. Within a year, TechVision had a fully autonomous R&D center, capable of driving innovation and supporting global projects without constant external assistance.

Impact on Your Business

Choosing the right service provider can significantly impact your business's success in India. It simplifies the setup process, reduces operational headaches, and allows you to focus on what you do best—growing your business. The right partner becomes your bridge to a new market, offering a strategic advantage that sets you apart from competitors.

Imagine launching your business in one of the world's most dynamic markets without the usual startup hiccups. With a reliable service provider, you gain access to local expertise, streamlined processes, and a faster route to market. This not only enhances your operational efficiency but also positions your business for sustainable growth and success.

In summary, partnering with a comprehensive service provider offers unparalleled convenience, saves time, and prepares you for independent operations in the future. It transforms the daunting task of setting up and operating in India into a smooth, manageable process, ensuring your business thrives in this promising market.

Overcoming Challenges

Common challenges and solutions

Setting up a business in India offers immense opportunities, but it comes with its own set of challenges. Here are three common challenges and practical solutions to overcome them by finding an all-in-one service provider.

Challenge 1: Navigating Complex Regulations

Problem: Indian regulations can be intricate, varying significantly across states and industries. Understanding and complying with these laws can be overwhelming for foreign business owners.

Solution: Partner with a comprehensive service provider who has local legal experts. They will navigate the regulations for you, ensuring compliance and preventing legal hassles, allowing you to focus on your business growth.

Challenge 2: Cultural and Communication Barriers

Problem: Differences in business culture and communication styles can lead to misunderstandings and inefficiencies. This is particularly challenging when managing a diverse workforce.

Solution: An all-in-one service provider offers cultural training and effective communication strategies. They can facilitate smooth interactions and help you build a cohesive team, ensuring your business operates harmoniously.

Challenge 3: Establishing a Reliable Supply Chain

Problem: Building a reliable supply chain in a new market can be daunting. Issues like logistics, vendor reliability, and inventory management need careful handling.

Solution: Comprehensive service providers offer supply chain management solutions, from selecting reliable vendors to ensuring timely logistics. They streamline these processes, ensuring your supply chain is efficient and resilient, helping your business run smoothly from day one.

Real-World Example: TechGrow

TechGrow, a U.S.-based tech company, faced similar challenges when expanding to India. They partnered with an all-in-one service provider who managed regulatory compliance, provided cultural training, and set up a robust supply chain. Within six months, TechGrow successfully launched their operations in India, benefiting from local expertise and a seamless setup process.

Best Practices

- Due Diligence: Research and choose a service provider with a proven track record in handling foreign businesses in India.
- Integrated Solutions: Opt for a provider offering end-to-end services to cover all aspects of your business needs.
- Local Expertise: Ensure the provider has strong local connections and knowledge to navigate the Indian business landscape efficiently.

By addressing these common challenges with the help of a reliable service provider, you can set up, operate, and grow your business in India smoothly and successfully.

Support Networks and Resources

Starting a business in India can seem like a big adventure, but having the right support networks and resources can make the journey much smoother. These networks offer extensive services that are super helpful for USA and European business owners looking to tap into India's amazing potential.

Local Expertise at Your Fingertips

Think of industry associations and local business councils as your go-to guides. They know the Indian market inside out and can help you with everything from understanding regulations to figuring out the best way to enter the market. For example, the Indo-American Chamber of Commerce (IACC) hosts seminars and workshops that can give you crucial insights about doing business in India.

Navigating Legal and Regulatory Waters

Dealing with legal stuff can be tricky, but support networks often include legal advisors who specialize in helping foreign businesses. These experts can assist with company registration, compliance issues, and other legal requirements, making sure your business stays on the right side of the law. This way, you can avoid legal headaches and focus on what you do best.

Finding and Keeping Top Talent

Getting the right people on your team is vital. Support networks often work with recruitment agencies and HR consultants who can help you attract top Indian talent. They know the local job market well and can help you create competitive compensation packages, effective recruitment strategies, and navigate Indian labor laws.

Boosting Operational Efficiency

Support networks provide access to resources that can make your operations run like a well-oiled machine. This includes supply chain experts, IT support, and facility management services. Partnering with a local IT firm, for example, can ensure your technological infrastructure is solid and secure, keeping your business running smoothly.

Best Practices

- Engage Early: Get in touch with support networks as soon as you decide to expand into India. Early engagement can offer valuable insights and help you avoid common mistakes.
- Utilize All Resources: Make the most of the resources available, from legal advice to networking events.
- Build Relationships: Develop relationships within these networks. Long-term partnerships can provide ongoing support and open doors to new opportunities.

By tapping into these support networks and resources, you can streamline the process of setting up your business in India, making the transition easier and setting a strong foundation for growth.

Chapter 8: Service Sector Excellence

India's Software and Technology Talent

India's expertise in software and technology

Success stories of global tech companies leveraging Indian talent

Collaborating with Indian Partners

Best practices for effective collaboration

Building strong, productive partnerships

India's Expertise in Software and Technology

India has earned a stellar reputation globally as a hub for software and technology talent. Over the years, the country has contributed significantly to the tech world, producing innovative solutions and nurturing top-tier professionals who have driven the digital transformation across industries. This subchapter provides an overview of India's expertise in software and technology, highlighting key contributions, renowned companies, and the professionalism that sets Indian tech talent apart.

India's Contributions to Global Tech Innovations

One of the most remarkable contributions India has made to the world is the Unified Payments Interface (UPI). Launched in 2016 by the National Payments Corporation of India (NPCI), UPI has revolutionized the fintech landscape. It allows users to transfer money instantly between bank accounts via mobile devices, without the need for banking details. This seamless and secure system has not only boosted financial inclusion in India but also garnered global interest, inspiring similar innovations in other countries.

Another area where India has excelled is in software development and IT services. Indian companies like Tata Consultancy Services (TCS), Infosys, and Wipro have become global leaders, providing cutting-edge solutions and services to clients worldwide. These firms have developed software that powers critical systems in various sectors, from banking and healthcare to retail and telecommunications. Their ability to deliver high-quality, cost-effective solutions has made India the go-to destination for software development and IT services.

Renowned Software Consultants and Developers

India is home to some of the most reputed software consultants and developers. TCS, for instance, is the largest IT services company in the world by market capitalization, serving clients in over 46 countries. Infosys, another giant in the industry, is known for its innovative approaches to digital transformation and consulting. Wipro, with its deep expertise in AI and cloud computing, has also made significant contributions to the tech industry.

These companies, among others, have set benchmarks for excellence in software development. They employ a vast pool of skilled professionals who are proficient in various programming languages, frameworks, and technologies. The rigorous training programs and continuous learning opportunities provided by these firms ensure that their employees stay ahead of the curve, adapting to the latest industry trends and technological advancements.

Professionalism and Work Ethic

Indian tech professionals are renowned for their excellent professionalism and strong work ethic. They are known for their dedication, problem-solving abilities, and collaborative approach to projects. The education system in India, with its emphasis on STEM (Science, Technology, Engineering, and Mathematics), produces graduates who are well-equipped to tackle complex technical challenges.

Moreover, Indian professionals are adept at working in multicultural environments. With English being a primary medium of instruction in most educational institutions, communication barriers are minimal when collaborating with international clients. This linguistic proficiency, combined with a deep understanding of global business practices, makes Indian tech talent highly desirable.

Well-Researched Facts

To understand the scale of India's tech prowess, consider these well-researched facts:

India is home to the second-largest developer community in the world, with over 3 million software developers.

The IT and BPM (Business Process Management) sector in India is expected to grow to $350 billion by 2025, according to a report by Nasscom.

Indian tech companies account for over 55% of the global outsourcing market.

These statistics underscore the significant role India plays in the global tech ecosystem. The country's ability to produce world-class software solutions and its vast pool of skilled professionals make it an indispensable player in the technology sector.

Best Practices for Leveraging Indian Tech Talent

- Engage with Reputed Firms: Partnering with established Indian tech companies like TCS, Infosys, or Wipro ensures access to top-notch expertise and reliable services.
- Invest in Long-Term Relationships: Building long-term relationships with Indian tech partners can lead to more customized solutions and better alignment with your business goals.
- Embrace Collaboration: Encourage collaborative projects and knowledge-sharing between your in-house team and Indian tech professionals to foster innovation and efficiency.

Real-World Impact

Consider the example of a European financial services firm that partnered with an Indian software company to develop a secure and user-friendly mobile banking app. By leveraging India's expertise in fintech, the firm was able to launch the app ahead of schedule, gaining a competitive edge in the market and significantly improving customer satisfaction.

In summary, India's software and technology sector is a powerhouse of innovation and expertise. From groundbreaking fintech solutions like UPI to the global influence of companies like TCS and Infosys, India continues to shape the future of technology. By tapping into this vast reservoir of talent and knowledge, USA and European business owners can drive their businesses forward, harnessing the full potential of Indian software and technology excellence.

Success Stories of Global Tech Companies Leveraging Indian Talent

India's software and technology talent has been a game-changer for numerous global tech companies. From Silicon Valley giants to European innovators, many have successfully tapped into India's vast pool of skilled professionals to drive their businesses forward. In this subchapter, we'll explore some impactful success stories that illustrate the profound impact of leveraging Indian talent.

The Google Story: Scaling Innovations

Google, one of the world's leading tech companies, has a significant presence in India. Sundar Pichai, Google's CEO, is a testament to the impact of Indian talent on the global stage. Under his leadership, Google has continued to innovate and expand its product offerings. Google's research and development centers in Bangalore and Hyderabad are pivotal in driving the company's global projects.

A key success story is the development of Google Pay. Initially launched as Tez in India, this payment app was designed specifically to cater to the unique needs of the Indian market. Leveraging the expertise of Indian engineers and their deep understanding of local consumer behavior, Google Pay quickly became a leading mobile payment platform in India. Its success in India paved the way for its global expansion, demonstrating how local insights can drive international success.

Microsoft: Empowering Digital Transformation

Microsoft has long recognized the potential of Indian talent. The company's largest R&D center outside the USA is in Hyderabad, employing thousands of engineers who contribute to core product development and innovation.

One notable success is the development of Microsoft's Azure cloud platform. Indian engineers played a crucial role in building and scaling Azure, which has become a cornerstone of Microsoft's business. Azure's growth is a direct result of the innovative work done in India, where engineers continuously improve cloud services, making them more reliable and efficient for users worldwide.

IBM: Driving Global Innovation

IBM has been leveraging Indian talent for decades, with a significant portion of its global workforce based in India. The company's Bangalore and Pune centers are key hubs for research and development, focusing on cutting-edge technologies like artificial intelligence (AI) and blockchain.

A standout success story is IBM's work with AI-driven healthcare solutions. Indian engineers and data scientists have been instrumental in developing IBM Watson Health, an AI platform that analyzes vast amounts of medical data to provide insights for better patient care. This technology is now used globally, showcasing how Indian talent can drive innovations that address critical global challenges.

Real-World Example: Kraft Heinz Global Capability Centre, Ahmedabad

Consider the journey of Kraft Heinz, the global food and beverage giant, which aimed to enhance its operations through its Global Capability Centre (GCC) in Ahmedabad. By leveraging Indian tech talent, Kraft Heinz was able to streamline its processes, enhance data analytics, and improve overall efficiency.

The GCC in Ahmedabad serves as a crucial hub for Kraft Heinz, providing support across various functions such as IT, finance, supply chain, and HR. Indian professionals at the center bring invaluable expertise in these areas, driving innovation and operational excellence.

Kraft Heinz's decision to establish the GCC in Ahmedabad was driven by the city's rich pool of skilled professionals and robust infrastructure. This strategic move has enabled the company to tap into local insights and expertise, significantly boosting its global operations.

Best Practices for Leveraging Indian Talent

- Establish Local R&D Centers: Setting up research and development centers in India allows companies to tap directly into the local talent pool. These centers can become innovation hubs that drive global projects.
- Foster Collaborative Cultures: Encourage cross-cultural collaboration by integrating Indian teams with global counterparts. This can lead to diverse perspectives and innovative solutions.

- Invest in Continuous Learning: Provide opportunities for ongoing training and professional development. Indian tech professionals value education and continuous improvement, which can significantly enhance their contributions.
- Leverage Local Insights: Utilize the deep understanding Indian professionals have of their own market to develop products that resonate locally and globally.

These success stories underscore the transformative impact of leveraging Indian talent. Global tech companies like Google, Microsoft, IBM, and Kraft Heinz have demonstrated that tapping into India's software and technology expertise can lead to groundbreaking innovations and substantial business growth. By establishing local R&D centers, fostering collaborative cultures, and investing in continuous learning, USA and European business owners can harness the full potential of Indian talent, driving their businesses to new heights.

Collaborating with Indian Partners

Best Practices for Effective Collaboration

Collaborating with Indian partners can be a game-changer for USA and European business owners looking to establish and grow their businesses in India. The right partner can provide a comprehensive range of services to help you navigate the complexities of the Indian market, streamline your operations, and set a strong foundation for growth. Here are some best practices for effective collaboration with Indian partners.

Understand the Cultural Nuances

The first step in successful collaboration is understanding the cultural nuances of doing business in India. Indian business culture emphasizes relationships and trust. Spend time building a rapport with your partners. Attend meetings, share meals, and show genuine interest in their perspectives. This relationship-building phase is crucial for establishing trust and mutual respect.

For example, an American tech startup, wanted to establish an R&D center in India. They invested time in understanding the cultural norms and practices, which helped them build a strong relationship with their Indian partners. This foundation of trust made subsequent collaborations smoother and more productive.

Clearly Define Roles and Responsibilities

Effective collaboration requires clarity in roles and responsibilities. Define what each party will handle to avoid overlaps and confusion. Use clear, concise language in your agreements and communications. This clarity helps ensure that everyone knows their duties and can focus on their tasks efficiently.

When a European pharmaceutical company, partnered with an Indian firm for manufacturing, they faced initial challenges due to unclear roles. Once they redefined their roles and responsibilities clearly, the collaboration improved significantly, leading to increased efficiency and output.

Regular Communication and Updates

Maintaining regular communication is key to a successful partnership. Schedule regular meetings to discuss progress, address issues, and plan next steps. Use multiple communication channels such as emails, video calls, and instant messaging to keep everyone in the loop. Transparency in communication builds trust and ensures that both parties are aligned with the project goals.

Leverage Local Expertise

One of the main advantages of partnering with an Indian firm is their local expertise. Leverage this knowledge to navigate regulatory requirements, cultural nuances, and market conditions. Your Indian partner can provide insights that are crucial for making informed decisions and avoiding common pitfalls.

For instance, a European fashion brand, relied on their Indian partner's expertise to understand local consumer preferences. This insight helped them tailor their products to the Indian market, leading to a successful launch and rapid growth.

Focus on Long-Term Goals

While short-term wins are important, focus on building a long-term partnership. This approach ensures sustained success and growth. Discuss your long-term goals with your partner and align your strategies to achieve them. A long-term perspective fosters loyalty and commitment from both parties.

Consider the case of an American software company. They entered a partnership with an Indian IT firm with a long-term vision. By focusing on strategic goals and continuously investing in their relationship, they built a strong, enduring partnership that drove innovation and growth for both companies.

Adaptability and Flexibility

India is a dynamic and diverse market. Be prepared to adapt and be flexible in your approach. Your Indian partner can guide you through the changing market conditions and help you pivot when necessary. Flexibility in your plans and operations can lead to better outcomes and resilience in the face of challenges.

A notable example is a European renewable energy company, which had to adapt their strategy due to regulatory changes in India. Their Indian partner's adaptability and local knowledge helped them navigate the changes smoothly, ensuring the project's success.

Effective collaboration with Indian partners involves understanding cultural nuances, clearly defining roles, maintaining regular communication, leveraging local expertise, focusing on long-term goals, and being adaptable. By following these best practices, USA and European business owners can build strong, productive partnerships that facilitate the successful establishment, operation, and growth of their businesses in India.

Through these collaborative efforts, you can harness the full potential of India's untapped talents and infrastructure, driving your business to new heights.

Building Strong, Productive Partnerships

Establishing your business in India offers immense opportunities but can be daunting without the right support. Partnering with an all-in-one service provider can streamline this process, offering a fast and convenient setup and helping you build a strong, productive partnership.

Simplified Setup Process

Imagine having a single partner handle everything from market research to office setup. This is the power of an all-in-one service provider. Take, for example, a U.S.-based tech company. When they decided to expand into India, they partnered with a comprehensive service provider who took care of all the logistics. This included securing the necessary licenses, setting up the IT infrastructure, and even recruiting local talent. As a result, Innovatech was operational in India within weeks, avoiding the usual bureaucratic delays.

Local Expertise and Deep Insights

An all-in-one service provider brings invaluable local expertise. They are familiar with the regulatory landscape, cultural nuances, and market dynamics. For instance, when, a European renewable energy company, entered the Indian market, their provider's deep understanding of local regulations and business practices was crucial. This expertise allowed to navigate complex compliance requirements smoothly, ensuring a hassle-free market entry.

Ongoing Support for Growth

A strong partnership means having support beyond the initial setup. An all-in-one service provider offers continuous services like HR management, supply chain logistics, and compliance monitoring. Consider MedHealth, a European pharmaceutical firm. Their provider's ongoing support with regulatory updates, talent management, and operational logistics allowed MedHealth to focus on innovation and expansion. This comprehensive support system enabled MedHealth to establish a robust presence in India and scale their operations effectively.

Partnering with an all-in-one service provider can significantly ease the process of establishing and growing your business in India. By leveraging their local expertise, streamlined processes, and comprehensive support, you can focus on what you do best—driving your business forward. Building a strong, productive partnership with the right provider not only saves time and resources but also sets a solid foundation for long-term success in the vibrant and dynamic Indian market.

Appendix A: Useful Resources

Links to Important Documents and Websites

Company Registration and Compliance

- Ministry of Corporate Affairs: mca.gov.in

Taxation and GST

- Central Board of Direct Taxes (CBDT): incometaxindia.gov.in
- Goods and Services Tax (GST): gst.gov.in

Intellectual Property Rights

- Intellectual Property India: ipindia.nic.in

Import and Export Regulations

- Directorate General of Foreign Trade (DGFT): dgft.gov.in

Labor Laws and Employee Benefits

- Ministry of Labour & Employment: labour.gov.in

Environmental Regulations

- Ministry of Environment, Forest and Climate Change: moef.gov.in

Additional Resources

Business Setup Guides

- India Entry Strategy Guide by Invest India
- Doing Business in India by PwC

Market Research and Reports

- NASSCOM Reports
- FICCI Research and Publications

Networking and Business Development

- CII Events and Conferences
- FICCI Events and Webinars

By leveraging these resources, USA and European business owners can access vital information, connect with key agencies, and utilize valuable tools to successfully establish and grow their businesses in India.

Appendix B: Checklist For Setting Up In India

Pre-Setup Phase

Conduct Market Research

- Identify target market and customer demographics.
- Analyze competitors and market trends.
- Evaluate the demand for your products/services.

Define Business Structure

- Choose the type of entity (e.g., private limited company, LLP, branch office).
- Draft a business plan with clear objectives and strategies.

Legal and Regulatory Requirements

- Consult with legal advisors for compliance.
- Register your business with the Ministry of Corporate Affairs (MCA).
- Obtain necessary licenses and permits specific to your industry.

Financial Planning

- Prepare a detailed financial plan and budget.
- Open a local bank account.
- Arrange for initial funding and working capital.

Location Selection

- Choose the city and specific location for your office or facility.
- Consider factors such as infrastructure, talent pool, and proximity to customers and suppliers.

Setup Phase

Office Space and Infrastructure

- Lease or purchase office space.
- Set up necessary infrastructure, including IT systems and furniture.
- Ensure compliance with local building and safety regulations.

Hiring and Staffing

- Recruit local talent or relocate existing employees.
- Set up HR policies and employee benefits.
- Arrange for employee training and development programs.

Technology and Systems

- Implement necessary IT systems and software.
- Ensure robust cybersecurity measures.
- Set up communication systems, including internet and phone lines.

Legal and Compliance

- Register for Goods and Services Tax (GST).
- Obtain necessary environmental, health, and safety approvals.
- Ensure compliance with labor laws and employment regulations.

Supply Chain and Logistics

- Identify and partner with local suppliers and vendors.
- Set up a reliable supply chain and logistics network.
- Establish inventory management systems.

Post-Setup Phase

Marketing and Sales

- Develop a marketing strategy tailored to the Indian market.

- Launch promotional campaigns and advertising.
- Establish a sales team and distribution channels.

Operational Management

- Set up standard operating procedures (SOPs) for daily operations.
- Implement quality control and assurance measures.
- Monitor performance and make necessary adjustments.

Financial Management

- Set up accounting and bookkeeping systems.
- Ensure regular financial reporting and audits.
- Monitor cash flow and manage expenses.

Continuous Improvement

- Collect feedback from customers and employees.
- Continuously improve products, services, and processes.
- Stay updated with market trends and regulatory changes.

Ongoing Support and Growth

Networking and Partnerships

- Join local industry associations and chambers of commerce.
- Build relationships with local businesses and government agencies.
- Attend networking events and business conferences.

Scalability and Expansion

- Plan for business scalability and future expansion.
- Explore new markets and business opportunities within India.
- Invest in research and development to innovate and stay competitive.

By following this comprehensive checklist, USA and European business owners can ensure a smooth and successful setup process in India, laying a strong foundation for long-term growth and success.

Appendix C: How Ascetic Business Solution Can Help

Ascetic Business Solution is your trusted partner in navigating the complexities of establishing and growing your business in India. We offer a comprehensive range of services designed to provide end-to-end support, ensuring a seamless and efficient setup process. Here's how we can assist you:

Market Research and Feasibility Studies

- In-Depth Market Analysis: We conduct thorough market research to help you understand the Indian business landscape, identify target markets, and analyze competitor strategies.
- Feasibility Studies: Assess the viability of your business idea in the Indian context, considering economic, technical, and legal factors.

Business Registration and Legal Compliance

- Business Entity Formation: Assist in selecting the right business structure and handling all aspects of company registration with the Ministry of Corporate Affairs (MCA).
- Regulatory Compliance: Ensure compliance with local regulations, including obtaining necessary licenses and permits.

Financial Planning and Taxation

- Financial Setup: Help you set up local bank accounts, arrange initial funding, and create a detailed financial plan.
- Taxation Advisory: Provide expert advice on tax planning, GST registration, and compliance to optimize your financial efficiency.

Location Selection and Office Setup

- Site Selection: Assist in choosing the optimal location for your office or facility based on your business needs.
- Office Setup: Manage the leasing or purchasing of office space and oversee the setup of infrastructure, including IT systems and furniture.

Talent Acquisition and HR Management

- Recruitment Services: Source and recruit top local talent to build a skilled and dedicated workforce.
- HR Policies and Training: Develop HR policies, administer employee benefits, and provide training and development programs.

Technology and IT Support

- IT Infrastructure: Implement robust IT systems and cybersecurity measures to support your operations.
- Software Solutions: Offer tailored software development and maintenance services to meet your business needs.

Supply Chain and Logistics Management

- Vendor Management: Identify and partner with reliable local suppliers and vendors.
- Logistics Solutions: Set up an efficient supply chain and logistics network to ensure smooth operations.

Marketing and Sales Support

- Marketing Strategy: Develop and execute a marketing strategy tailored to the Indian market, including digital marketing and advertising campaigns.
- Sales Development: Establish a sales team and distribution channels to effectively reach your target customers.

Ongoing Operational Support

- Operational Management: Set up standard operating procedures (SOPs) and implement quality control measures.
- Financial Management: Provide ongoing accounting and bookkeeping services, regular financial reporting, and audit support.

Continuous Improvement and Growth

- Feedback and Improvement: Collect and analyze feedback to continuously improve products, services, and processes.
- Expansion Planning: Assist in planning for scalability and exploring new market opportunities within India.

Why Choose Ascetic Business Solution?

- Expertise: Extensive knowledge of the Indian market and regulatory environment.
- Comprehensive Services: End-to-end solutions tailored to meet your specific business needs.
- Local Network: Strong connections with local businesses, government agencies, and industry associations.
- Commitment to Excellence: Dedicated to providing high-quality services that drive your business success.

By partnering with Ascetic Business Solution, you can navigate the complexities of the Indian market with confidence and achieve sustainable growth. Let us help you harness the full potential of India's untapped talents and infrastructure to propel your business to new heights.

Conclusion: Your Journey Begins Now

India is the ideal destination for IT services, offering unparalleled talent, cost-efficiency, and innovative solutions. Key takeaways include leveraging India's vast skilled workforce, benefiting from lower operational costs, and tapping into a culture of innovation. By partnering with the right Indian business service provider, you can seamlessly navigate the complexities of setting up and growing your business.

Embrace this opportunity to harness India's potential, drive your business forward, and achieve new heights in the global market. Your journey to success in India begins now. Partner with a trusted Indian business service provider to ensure a smooth transition and sustained growth. Their local expertise and comprehensive support can help you overcome challenges and capitalize on opportunities. Remember, the right partner will not only assist you in setting up your business but will also empower you to thrive and innovate in the vibrant Indian market. Take the leap and start your journey today.

About Authors

Riken Bhorania

Riken Bhorania has been working with hundreds of EU and US business owners to help them provide services from India since 2009 to improve productivity and business process optimization. His expertise in setting up and scaling teams in India for EU and US business owners brings excellent returns on clients' investments. Hundreds of assignments have been taken care of by Ascetic Business Solution, and Riken is one of the co-founders of Ascetic Business Solution. He aims to share awareness and implement the strategy for EU and US business owners to leverage India's talents and ensure long-term sustainability with quality IT and Business Operations.

Bhaumin Chorera

Bhaumin Chorera is the co-founder of Ascetic Business Solution and drives the tech and business process setup of the team. His keen attention to detail and client success approach help EU and US business owners implement effective strategies. After working on hundreds of assignments, he knows what would be best for scaling any specific type of technology business in India. He is a master of people, processes, and technology. Under his guidance, many people have created great careers, and he has served many business owners worldwide. Bhaumin is known for his process-driven, result-oriented attitude that brings key advantages to all stakeholders.

- *You can contact them at contact@asceticbs.com*